AF251899

Criminal Justice
Recent Scholarship

Edited by
Nicholas P. Lovrich

A Series from LFB Scholarly

ARRESTED ADOLESCENT OFFENDERS
A Study of Delayed Transitions to Adulthood

Christopher Salvatore

LFB Scholarly Publishing LLC
El Paso 2013

Library of Congress Cataloging-in-Publication Data

Salvatore, Christopher, 1974-
  Arrested adolescent offenders : a study of delayed transitions to adulthood / Christopher Salvatore.
      pages cm. -- (Criminal justice: recent scholarship)
  Includes bibliographical references and index.
  ISBN 978-1-59332-591-6 (hbk. : alk. paper)
  1. Juvenile delinquents. 2. Adolescence. 3. Adulthood. I. Title.
  HV9069.S244 2013
  364.36--dc23
                                              2012051143

ISBN 978-1-59332-591-6

The author would like to thank the faculty and staff of the Department of Criminal Justice at Temple University in Philadelphia Pennsylvania for their guidance and support through this project.

Table of Contents

CHAPTER 1

Emerging Adulthood

The journey to adulthood has drastically changed in the United States and other developed nations over the last 50 years (Cote, 2000; Okimoto & Stegall, 1987). The transition period between adolescence and adulthood has become longer as marriage and parenthood, traditional markers of adulthood, have been postponed and many people have extended their education, training and self-exploration into their twenties (Arnett, 1998, 2000; Cote, 2000). This stage of the life course has been identified as *emerging adulthood* (Arnett, 1998, 2000, 2001, 2005, 2006), a period lasting from about age 18 to 25- although for many it can extend through the twenties and thirties. Many in emerging adulthood have high rates of risky behavior and engage in acts of delinquency usually seen among adolescents. In this study, I examine how this new stage of the life course has had unique age and period effects on recent generations, influencing criminal offending by extending the active period for low-level offenders who traditionally peak earlier in the "age crime curve" and creating a new offender type, the arrested adolescent.

The age crime curve refers to the age distribution of crime. Benson (2002) described the age crime curve as having an inverse j pattern. The onset of criminality is typically around age 10, offending peaks between the ages of 15 and 19, and then gradually declines until about age 55 where the age-adjusted rate of criminality is close to zero.

Through an extensive program of research (Moffitt, 1993; Moffitt, Caspi, Rutter, & Silva, 2001; Moffitt, 2006), Moffitt has identified a developmental taxonomy that classifies several different types of offenders. One type is the "adolescent limited" (AL) offender, who commits low-level crimes during the teenage years (e.g., shoplifting, public disorder), and whose offending decreases as he "ages out" of adolescence and reaches traditional life course turning points (Moffitt, 1993).[1] ALs offending is rooted in role confusion during adolescence, due to a gap between biological maturity and culturally defined maturity. Many respond to this confusion by committing low-level offenses. More serious offenders, known as life course persistent (LCPs) offenders are also active in adolescence. Table 1 presents a brief summary of the offender typologies Moffitt includes in her taxonomy and "adds" the arrested adolescent offender to these types.

As members of the AL group transition through emerging adulthood (about ages 18-25), they either successfully reach culturally defined turning points (e.g., marriage) that increase social bonds and decrease offending, or they fail to reach these turning points and continue to offend as low level "arrested adolescent" (AAO) offenders. AAO's are, in essence, older ALs who failed to make successful on-time transitions to adult roles. He or she has the same background characteristics and offending patterns as the adolescent limited offender. However, unlike Moffitt's AL, the arrested adolescent does not desist as quickly because of failure to enter adult social roles. The more serious LCPs will continue to offend, committing more serious, predatory offenses. Because of the impact of various social and psychological factors, turning points will not have the same influence on LCPs as they do on ALs.

The purpose of this study is to examine whether a new stage of the life course, emerging adulthood, is influencing offending trajectories by extending the period of active offending for some adolescent limited offenders. Because emerging adulthood delays many of these traditional turning points (Arnett, 2005), here I argue that some ALs may continue to offend as "arrested adolescent offenders" (AAOs) (see Table 1). Implications for both criminal justice policy and criminological theory are discussed below.

---

[1] The concept "turning points" has been defined by Elder (1998) as a "dramatic change in (their) life course" (p.8). Turning points can include marriage, having children, and military service. Turning points increase social bonds in adulthood and attachments are built that inhibit crime and deviance (Laub & Sampson, 1993).

Table 1.   *Key Identifiers: Offender subgroup by life course stage*

Offender subgroup	Stage of Life Course		
	Add Health Wave 1 - Adolescence (1995) Age range= 11-18 Mean=16	**Add Health Wave 2 - Adolescence (1996) Age range = 12-18 Mean=16**	**Add Health Wave 3 - Emerging Adulthood (2001-2002) Age range =18-25 Mean=22**
Abstainers	Crime: None Social bonds: Good Turning points: No Neuro-psychological deficits: No	Crime: None Social bonds: Good Turning points: Transitioning Neuro-psychological deficits: No	Crime: None Social bonds: Good Turning points: On time Neuro-psychological deficits: No
AL	Crime: Low level Social bonds: OK Turning points: No Neuro-psychological deficits: No	Crime: Low level Social bonds: OK Turning points: Transitioning Neuro-psychological deficits: No	Crime: None Social bonds: Good Turning points: On time Neuro-psychological deficits: No
AAO	(AL at Wave 1) Crime: Low level Social bonds: OK Turning points: No Neuro-psychological deficits: No	(AL at Wave 2) Crime: Low level Social bonds: OK Turning points: No Neuro-psychological deficits: No	Crime: Low level Social bonds: Weaker Turning points: Delayed Neuro-psychological deficits: No
LCP	Crime: Serious Social bonds: Poor Turning points: No Neuro-psychological deficits: Yes	Crime: Serious Social bonds: Poor Turning points: No Neuro-psychological deficits: Yes	Crime: Serious Social bonds: Poor Turning points: Absent Neuro-psychological deficits: Yes

CRIMINAL JUSTICE POLICY IMPLICATIONS

The modern juvenile justice system has evolved over the last fifty years to deal with the unique challenges of youths who commit criminal offenses, as well as those presented by juveniles who have been identified as delinquent and taken into state custody (Marion & Oliver, 2006). Consisting of thousands of agencies at the federal and state levels, juvenile justice agencies deal with offenders who are younger than the age of eighteen (Fagin, 2007). The majority of offenses committed by adolescents are non-index offenses (e.g., disorderly conduct, vandalism) (Marion & Oliver, 2006, p. 432) and most meet the criteria identified by Moffitt (1993) as adolescent limited offenders; that is, they engage in low level offending during adolescence but "age out" as they transition to traditional social roles (e.g., full-time employment, marriage) that inhibit offending.

The shift in criminal justice policy from the due process model that focused on the protection of individual liberties to the crime control model that focuses more on halting criminal behavior has resulted in increasingly punitive punishments for all offenders including juveniles (Aloisi, 2000). Despite the fact that most juvenile offenders primarily commit low-level offenses, as these offenders age into emerging adulthood some may continue to commit these offenses as arrested adolescent offenders while no longer under the jurisdiction of the juvenile justice system.As "adult" criminals, arrested adolescent offenders are subject to criminal trials or, in most cases, plea bargains (Champion, Hartley, & Rabe, 2008). Arrested adolescent offenders could create several challenges for the criminal justice system. First, an increase in adults committing low-level offenses more typical of adolescents may increase operating expenses of courts and correctional institutions. In addition, an influx of arrested adolescent offenders experimenting with low-level drug use may require the criminal justice system to expand its network of drug treatment programs (e.g., therapeutic communities, drug courts) that service drug offenders. Finally, arrested adolescent offenders who are incarcerated would invariably be exposed to the criminogenic effects of incarceration as well as the long term stigma commonly reported by former offenders (Laub & Sampson, 2003), thus limiting their potential for positive future social and occupational opportunities.

In addition to the criminal justice system other social institutions, particularly colleges and universities, may be affected by arrested adolescent offenders. Courts have recognized that students may need protection from injuries that result from hazing and other activities that frequently occur on campuses (Peters, 2007). As emerging adults attend college, many will participate in risky and dangerous behaviors that may increase the burden on institutional disciplinary committees, force institutions to intensify security and campus police presence, and add counseling and drug treatment services.

IMPLICATIONS FOR THEORY

The hypothesis that emerging adulthood extends the period of active offending**Error! Bookmark not defined.** through "arrested adolescence" may also have theoretical implications for the changing roles of social bonds and turning points in our culture. Hirschi (1969) argued that social bonds with parents, peers, and school, as well as commitment to conventional society could act to inhibit crime. Emerging adulthood, as presented by Arnett (1998), argues that society has changed and traditional bonds may not exist or operate as they had in the past. My efforts to show how a lack of social bonding can extend offending for some low-level offenders could help clarify the theoretical relationship between social bonds and offending for young people today who face a different set of social and cultural circumstances than prior generations.

This study also may have implications for life course theory that focuses on the role of time, social context, and process by considering historical events and changes as well as individual lives (Elder, 1985; Benson, 2002). Arnett's theory argues that traditional trajectories are delayed or postponed because of social and economic changes that have lead to an increased need for higher levels of education and a delay in entering the employment market (Arnett, 2005). This can lead to a delay in transitions and disrupt the development of social bonds that act to inhibit crime and deviance. This study explores how emerging adulthood has altered trajectories, and how this in turn affects offending. Study findings suggest that several turning points and social bonds were indeed related to offending and drug use during emerging adulthood.

FUTURE AREAS OF STUDY

Findings of this research have significant potential for advancing our understanding of the "age crime curve." Although the intention of this study is not to attempt to test hypotheses about the age-crime curve, greater insight into the relationship between age and crime may add to the growing body of knowledge related to emerging adulthood. Such insight has implications for early interventions, finding effective treatments for offenders, and identifying what factors lead to desistance.

There are two main schools of thought in the age-crime debate. The first is represented by Gottfredson and Hirschi (1990) who posit that the age-crime curve is invariant, having no variation across historical period, geographic location, or other cultural factors. The second viewpoint is that the age-crime curve does demonstrate variance in factors such as gender and type of crime (Moffitt et al., 2001; Moffitt 1993; Steffensmeier, Anderson, Harer, Streifel 1989; Farrington, 1986).

The hypothesis that emerging adulthood extends the period of active offending resulting in "arrested adolescence" is in contrast to Gottfredson and Hirschi's invariance argument as emerging adulthood is the result of unique economic, social, and historical circumstances that have caused the delay of traditional turning points. As such, the argument that emerging adulthood extends the period of active criminality for low-level offender's challenges the view that there is no variation in the relationship between age and crime across gender, racial groups, and type of crime.

SUMMARY AND A LOOK AHEAD

Emerging adulthood is a new stage of the life course that has the potential to alter the offending patterns of low-level offenders by delaying traditional turning points and altering social bonds. Arnett (2000) argued that due to the delay of turning points during emerging adulthood, many will participate in risky and dangerous behaviors including drug use and offending. The literature examining the role of emerging adulthood and crime and deviance (detailed in the following chapter) has provided a great deal of insight into how emerging adulthood has evolved as a unique stage of the life course, as well as its role in offending. Arnett's theory, however, has not been examined explicitly in the life course criminological literature.

The following analysis advances the understanding of the relationship of traditional social bonds and turning points for a cohort of individuals during emerging adulthood. The next chapter presents the relevant literature examining emerging adulthood and then focuses on the social changes that have brought about emerging adulthood. The research examining risky behaviors and drug use are then explored. Finally, the arrested adolescent offender is introduced in the context of existing offender taxonomies. Chapter three then discusses the data used for this study and the statistical methodology employed to test the key hypotheses of the study. Chapter four presents bivariate and multivariate results. Chapter five places the results within the framework of life course literature, and discusses findings that are both predicted and unexpected based on theoretical predictions, and concludes with limitations of the study and directions indicated for future research.

CHAPTER 2

Emerging Adulthood & Crime

Most research dealing with emerging adulthood has focused mainly on risky behaviors, such as reckless driving, substance use, and dangerous sexual behaviors (Arnett, 1998; Arnett, 2005; Chasin, Pitts, & Prost, 2002; Rohrbach, Sussmann, Dent, & Sun, 2005; Tucker, Ellickson, Orlando, Martino, & Klein, 2005; White, Labouvie, & Papadaratsakis, 2005), but little has been done to explore the genesis of crime during emergent adulthood (Piquero, Brame, Mazerolle, & Haapanen, 2002).

The term "arrested adolescent offender" is intended to describe a person who has failed to make "on-time" life course transitions (normatively defined as "age appropriate" transitions) or meet turning points in trajectories that mark the entrance into adulthood (Thornberry, 1997; Benson, 2002). Life course research has shown for the first half of the twentieth century in Western culture, transitions into adulthood included completion of formal education, getting a job, marrying, and having a family, and this typically occurred during one's late teens and early twenties (Arnett, 2000; Cote, 2000; Okimoto & Stegall, 1987).

More recently, however, changes in social and cultural structures of industrialized nations have contributed to a delay in the timing of many traditional turning points. These changes have included the decline of well paying manufacturing jobs, increases in low paying service positions, a shift to a credential-based employment market, and a rise in the number of people earning post-high school education (Cote & Allahar, 1995). Prior generations had access to a wide variety of employment opportunities that offered the prospect of a comfortable life with only a high school diploma. No longer having access to these positions, more recent generations have been forced to secure greater levels of education and experience to achieve employment that is typically of lower prestige and lower pay than prior generations (Cote

& Allahar, 1995, pp. 45-47). Those who make these transitions (e.g., completing education) between the ages of 18-25 are considered *on time* (Cote, 2000; Elder, 1985), and those made either before or after are considered *off time* (Thornberry, 1997). Those who make *on time* transitions meet normatively defined turning points (e.g., marriage, college, children, and full-time employment)[2] symbolizing successful entry into adulthood. Those who fail or delay these turning points often take several additional years to reach them and fully assimilate into adulthood (Cote, 2000).

In the pages that follow, the origin of emerging adulthood as a distinct stage of the life course with be examined, the role of risky behaviors and crime in emerging adulthood will be discussed, the justification for identifying a new category of offender, the arrested adolescent offender (AAO),will be presented, and existing research in the life course perspective will be used as the basis to propose a core hypothesis namely that those who fail to successfully transition to adult roles continue offending as AAOs participating in low level offenses.

THE EVOLUTION OF EMERGING ADULTHOOD

Possibly, one of the most significant perspectives to emerge recently in the field of developmental social psychology is the theory of emerging adulthood, proposed by Dr. Jeffrey Arnett (Arnett, 1998). Basically, Arnett's theory argues that emerging adulthood is a new stage of the life course — neither adolescence nor young adulthood— that is the byproduct of several types of social changes over the past 50 years. During emerging adulthood, many adult commitments and responsibilities are postponed, providing "emerging adults" with the opportunity to explore their identities and attitudes in the areas of romantic relationships, work, and worldview. Relying heavily on the concept of informal social control, he states that emerging adults' risk behaviors (e.g., drug use) can be explained as part of the identity

---

[2] It is possible that divorce could also act as a negative turning point towards offending as the sample ages. Future studies may want to include hypotheses examining the role of divorce as a turning point. It should also be noted that Moffitt (1993) and Moffitt et al. (2001) stated that early parenthood could act as a 'snare' and act as a risk factor for young people. However, early parenthood would most likely be a risk factor when individuals are in early/mid adolescence (at waves 1 and 2 in this sample).

exploration that would have been constrained and monitored by parents. Once married, they are further constrained from participation in risk behaviors because of the responsibilities of marriage and family (Arnett, 2000).

Arnett's concept of the impact of powerful, informal social controls has provided the foundation for several major studies of the influence of these controls on patterns of delinquency and criminality across the life course trajectory (Laub & Sampson, 2003; Moffitt et al., 2001). In the early stages of the life course, these controls are identified as primary agents of social control— namely, the family, school, and peers. As people mature to adulthood, marriage and employment become the dominant agents of social control (Benson, 2002; Laub & Sampson, 2003; Guo, Reottger, & Cai, 2008).

The concept of emerging adulthood presents a challenge to life course theorists by positing changes in the life course between adolescence and adulthood through which traditional bonds and attachments formed through marriage and employment are postponed. I argue that individuals without these bonds and attachments may drift into a period of "arrested adolescence" where they have reached biological maturation but fail to meet turning points that mark adulthood and create social bonds that inhibit deviance.

Life course theorists have noted that several major social and historical changes have led to emerging adulthood as a distinct stage of the life course (Arnett, 1998; 2000; 2005, Cote, 2000). First, as early as the 1960s, an increasing delay in the timing of marriage was evident (Espenshade, 1985) (see Figure 1). Both men and women in the U.S. began delaying marriage until they were older or chose not marry. For example, in 1987, 60.8% of women aged 20-24 had never married compared to 36.4 % in 1972 for the same age group. This trend is evident for men in this age group as well, with 77.7% of males never married in 1987, relative to 56.9% in 1972 (U.S. Bureau of Census, 1972, 1987).

Figure 1.   *Age of first marriage 1950-2000*

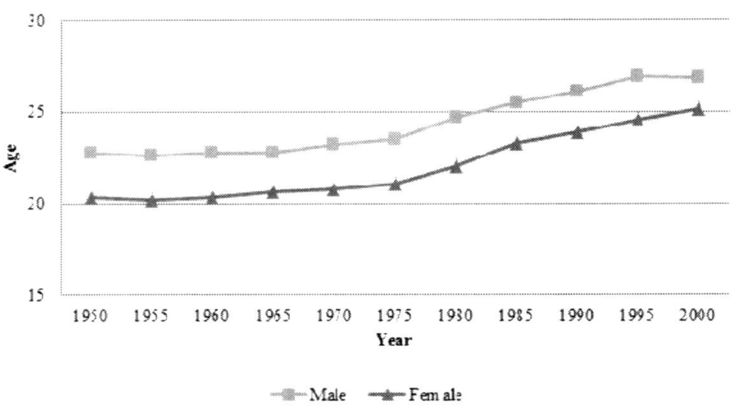

Source: Census Bureau,
http://www.census.gov/population/www/socdemo/hh-fam.html

Similarly, studies have shown that first-time parenthood has also been delayed (Wilkie, 1981). For example, Baldwin and Nord (1984) found that between 1970 and 1982 there was a marked increase in the age of women having their first children, with the biggest increase for women aged 30-34 years.

Finally, emerging adults no longer have the same prospects for earning enough money to support a "middle class" lifestyle without post high school education and training (Arnett, 2000; Cote, 2000; Cote & Allahar, 1995; Okimoto & Stegall, 1987). The need for higher-level education has been shown to be the result of the shift from a manufacturing to service-based economy (Burtless, 1990). In the early part of the twentieth century, most young Americans worked on family farms or gained employment in the manufacturing industry (Mirel, 1991). However, as the economy moved away from manufacturing towards a service-based economy, young people were faced with "education inflation," a need for increased credentials to attain adequate employment (Cote & Allahar, 1995). For example, by the mid-1980s, 75 percent of about 22.5 million college graduates were employed in occupations that typically call for a college-level degree (Sargent, 1986).

As noted above, marriage is considered one of the key transitions to adulthood, acting as a socializing institution that requires conformity to conventional social norms and lessens deviant behaviors such as drug and alcohol use (Arnett, 1998; Cote, 2000; Laub & Sampson, 2003). Prior research examined family role transitions (marriage and parenthood) in relation to risky behaviors (risky driving, substance abuse, and dangerous sexual behavior), finding that being married and having a child were related to reduced participation in these risky behaviors (Arnett, 1998). Moreover, many studies have found that those not married by their early twenties have a greater likelihood of engaging in criminal and dangerous behaviors (Chassin et al., 2002; Laub & Sampson, 2003; & White et al., 2005).

Like marriage, parenthood acts as a socializing institution, requiring avoidance of behaviors that endanger the lives of self or others (Arnett, 2001; Laub & Sampson, 2003). Laub and Sampson (2003) found that a significant number of the males they studied felt being a parent called for taking on adult responsibilities and allowed for less recreational time with peers. Previous research found that along with marriage, parenthood acts as a role transition causing an inverse correlation with deviant behaviors. Those who do not have children have a greater likelihood of engaging in criminal and delinquent behaviors (Arnett, 1998; Chassin et al., 2002; Laub & Sampson, 2003; Tucker et al., 2005; White et al., 2005).

In addition to marriage and parenthood, military service also has been identified as a life course turning point away from crime (Laub & Sampson, 1993, 2003). Laub and Sampson found that such service affected life course trajectories through three distinct processes. First, the military re-socializes, nullifying past failures and accomplishments alike, "knifing off" past experiences and reorganizing social roles. Next, the military provided training and educational opportunities, both in-and post-service through the G.I. Bill, increasing social capital which acts to increase attachments to employment and marriage. Finally, the military alters routine activities, and provides a structured environment with direct supervision and support (Laub & Sampson, 2003, pp. 48-51). This provided many of the men in their sample with an opportunity to reshape their social identities. The role of the military as a turning point can have negative consequences as well, as Wright, Carter, & Cullen (2005) found that most research studying the effectiveness of the military as a turning point away from crime mainly focused on veterans of World War II. Their study, in contrast to Laub and Sampson's (2003), used Vietnam veterans and found that service in Vietnam increased drug use. Thus, the inclusion of military service in the present study may provide clarification on how military service operates as a turning point in more recent cohorts.

The final area of cultural change discussed by Arnett is the economy. Starting in the 1970's the United States experienced a substantial increase in overall earnings inequality and in educational salary differentials. As a result, those with lower levels of education experienced large declines in earnings (Katz, 1994). For example, the William T. Grant Foundation (1988) reported that from 1973 through 1986 young males across all races and education levels experienced an average decline in economic prospects of 26 percent. For college graduates, salaries decreased only 6 percent between 1973 and 1986, relative to those with less than high school, who faced a decrease of 42 percent (William T. Grant Foundation, 1988). The cost of living in the United States increased significantly between the late 1960s and the early 1980s as reflected in the cost of tuition, apartment rents, homes, automobiles, and general household expenses (Okimoto & Stegall, 1987). For example, the consumer price index, a measure of money paid by urban residents for basic goods and services, showed a marked series of increases from 1960 through the 1980s (e.g., 1.6% in 1965, 5.7% in 1970, 9.1% in 1975, 13.5% in 1980, and 3.6% in 1985) (Bureau of Labor Statistics, 2008). Higher cost of living led many young people to postpone leaving home or resulted in a return home after living independently because of the inability to be financially independent.

Goldscheider & Goldscheider (1994) found that from the 1920s to the 1980s the rate of young adults returning home increased from 22 percent to almost 40 percent because of the difficulty in keeping an independent residence, a trend that continues to the present (Arnett, 2000; Cote, 2000). Leaving home is one of the key criteria for the transition to adulthood (Arnett, 2000). Living with either parent into ones' mid-twenties represents a delay in reaching adult status. The increased cost of living and education has forced more young people to postpone the customary turning points of leaving home, marriage, completion of education, and having children until they are financially independent (Cote & Allahar, 1995).

Historically, the average age of leaving home had declined from World War II until the 1960s, with white males leaving home at age 23.4 in 1950 and age 18.5 in 1960 (Gutman, Pinonm, & Pullum, 2002).

By 1970 through the 1990s, the average age of leaving home rose, with white males leaving home at age 20.4 in 1970, and age 21.7 in 1990 (Gutman, Pinon, & Pullman, 2002). In addition to leaving home at earlier ages, emerging adults have also had the highest rate of residential changes of any group. Goldscheider & Goldscheider (1994) found that almost 40 percent of emerging adults return to and leave their parents' home at least once during emerging adulthood. These lifestyle changes reflect the exploratory nature of emerging adulthood, usually coinciding with the beginning or end of a relationship, entering or leaving college, and starting or quitting a new job (Arnett, 2000, pp. 473-475). Likewise, higher education is pursued in a nonlinear fashion, with many working full or part-time jobs while in college (Arnett, 2000).

Figure 2.   *Rate of college enrollment of recent high school completers 1960-2000 (numbers in thousands)*

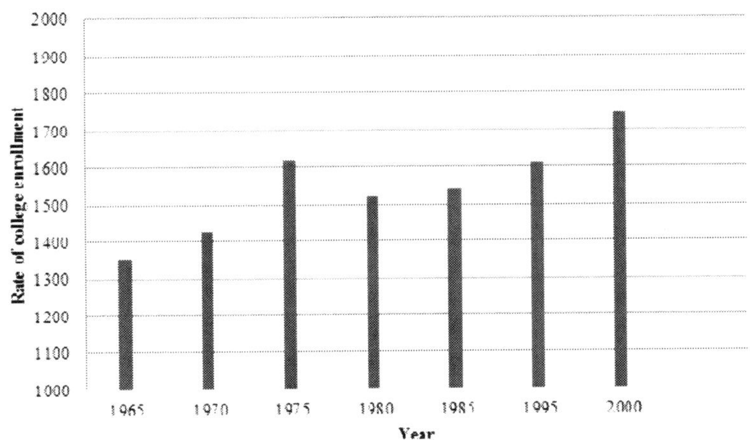

Source: National Center for Education Statistics,
http://nces.ed.gov/programs/digest/d05/tables/dt05_181.asp

In sum, emerging adulthood has been identified as a new stage of the life course resulting from the intersection of several socio-demographic and economic changes over the past 50 years, including the timing of marriage and parenthood, an overall increase in the cost of living, decreases in wages, education inflation, and an increase in the age at which individuals live independently. Many of those who have experienced emerging adulthood delay various turning points that would usually decrease deviant and criminal behavior. As a result, many in emerging adulthood are caught in a period of "arrested adolescence" in which low-level offending, typically seen in teenagers, continues.

RISKY BEHAVIORS, CRIME, & DEVIANCE IN EMERGING ADULTHOOD

One of the defining characteristics of being in emerging adulthood is a greater likelihood of engaging in high rates of risky and delinquent behaviors usually seen in adolescence. Prior research has found that dangerous behaviors (e.g., smoking, risky driving, binge drinking, drug use, and unsafe sexual behaviors) are highly prevalent during emerging adulthood (Arnett, 1998; Tucker et al., 2005; White, McMorris, Catalano, Fleming, Haggerty, & Abott, 2006; White & Jackson, 2004). Transitions (or lack thereof) during emerging adulthood have been found to influence participation in risky and dangerous behaviors (White et al., 2006). For example, White & Jackson (2005) examined the effects of the transition from adolescence to adulthood on drinking behaviors, finding that moving away from the controls of high school and leaving the parental home was related to higher rates of heavy drinking and alcohol- related problems in emerging adults.

Research in the area of risk behavior has traditionally focused on exploring these problems in adolescent populations (Hirschi, 1969; Bell & Bell, 1991; Jessor, Donovan, & Costa, 1991; Moffitt et al., 2001). More recently, studies have started to focus on increased risk behaviors during the period from adolescence to emerging adulthood (Chassin et al., 2002; Chen & Kandel, 1995; Rorhbach et al., 2005), and the period marking the onset and end of emerging adulthood (Shifren, Furnham, & Bauserman, 2003; White & Jackson, 2005). For example, Rohrbach et al., (2005) studied rates of tobacco, alcohol, and other drug use in a sample of alternative high school students for a five-year period from adolescence to emerging adulthood, finding that those who met traditional turning points (e.g., being married at the five year follow up) were less likely to use tobacco, alcohol, and marijuana. In another study, White & Jackson (2005) argued that the instability of emerging adulthood in the areas of education, residence, romantic relationships, and employment, accompanied by decreased levels of parental monitoring leads to increased alcohol use.

Arnett (2005) argued that increased substance abuse and risky behaviors during emerging adulthood are the result of increased freedom and reduced social controls. During the period of emerging adulthood, increasing instability and stress influence increases in rates of alcohol and drug use (Arnett, 2005). Without the informal social controls and attachments built through *on-time* transitions to marriage, family, and employment, those in emerging adulthood have fewer social bonds which act to inhibit risky, deviant, and criminal behaviors.

The motivation most often found in various forms of risky behavior is sensation seeking, the need for new and intense sensory experiences (Arnett, 1994). Those who are high in sensation seeking want to experience a high degree of novel and intense experiences, finding them pleasurable. Dangerous behaviors provide the novelty and stimulation that people who are high in sensation seeking desire. Arnett (1998) provides several examples of such sensation seeking behaviors, including driving a car at high speeds and sexual experimentation with multiple partners. Other factors that influence risky and criminal behaviors in emerging adults include an optimistic attitude, identity exploration, peer influence, and decreased parental monitoring (Arnett, 2005; White & Jackson, 2005).

Arnett (2005) states that an optimistic attitude is a common trait in emerging adults, and because of this attitude many persons in emerging adulthood do not view themselves as vulnerable to the potential dangers association with risky behaviors. Thus, emerging adults are more likely than others to drink excessively or engage in risky behaviors (Arnett, 2005). For example, emerging adults only see the benefits of alcohol consumption (i.e., having fun), but fail to see the negative effects (i.e., being arrested for drunk driving, developing alcoholism).

Another area identified by Arnett (2005) is identity exploration in the areas of love and work that largely occur in emerging adulthood rather than in adolescence (Arnett, 2005). Adolescence is when many have their first relationships and sexual experiences, but it is during emerging adulthood that people start to explore themselves on a deeper level to discover what type of qualities they are looking for in a romantic partner, as well as what type of long term employment they want to pursue (Arnett, 2005).

Identity exploration may relate to substance abuse and other dangerous behaviors in two specific ways. First, many emerging adults want to have various life experiences before they "settle down" into adult life; this can include experimentation with substance abuse (Arnett, 2005). Second, the process of developing an adult identity can be stressful and challenging (Arnett, 2005). Many in emerging adulthood may resort to substance abuse as a coping mechanism to deal with this stress (Arnett, 2005).

As emerging adults enter college or join the workforce, they may be vulnerable to peer influence because of their need to make new friendships (White & Jackson, 2005). Drinking lowers social inhibitions and promotes interacting with new peers (White & Jackson, 2005). Several studies have found that college students may drink more because of perceived attitudes than their own and norms on campus, with many students believing that campus attitudes are more permissive and that other students drink more than they actually do (Borsari & Carey, 2001, 2003).

The final area identified by Arnett (2005) is the role of parental monitoring. As individuals transition from adolescence to emerging adulthood parental monitoring decreases, and parents have less influence on dangerous and risky behaviors (White & Jackson, 2005). The relationship between parental oversight and substance abuse was examined systematically by Kypri, McCarthy, Coe, & Brown (2004). They found that rates of substance abuse increase in the year after high school as adolescents transitioned to emerging adulthood and moved out of their parent's home and levels of parental monitoring decreased. In the following year as many emerging adults left college dormitories and moved away from the monitoring of college residency, rates of substance abuse increased (Kypri et al., 2004). Thus, as emerging adults move away from parental and/or college dormitory monitoring they are subjected to fewer social controls and rates of substance abuse increase.

Turning to the role of crime in emerging adulthood, Piquero et al., (2002) examined the impact of emergent adulthood on criminal activity of male parolees released from the California Youth Authority between the ages of 21 and 28. Piquero and his colleagues found that arrest rates for both nonviolent and violent offenses peak in the early 20s during the period of emergent adulthood. The results of this study are in contrast to other researchers (viz., Gottfredson & Hirschi, 1990) who have argued the peak period to be in the mid to late teens.

THE ARRESTED ADOLESCENT OFFENDER

Drawing mainly on the work of Moffitt (1993) and Moffitt, Caspi, Rutter, & Silva (2001), the arrested adolescent offender is a descriptive category that is best understood in relation to the primary offender typology described through this research: adolescent limited offenders (ALs), which make up most offenders, and the life course persistent offenders (LCPs), a smaller and more serious group.

The AL offenders have mostly normal and healthy childhood backgrounds. Their antisocial behavior coincides with puberty and is largely the result of the "maturity gap" that Moffitt (1993) describes as the state of confusion experienced between biological maturation and transitioning into the adult world by means of access to mature privileges and responsibilities. Confusion stems from the fact that adolescents are biologically mature, but still are restricted from full participation in adult life (e.g., being able to vote, legally purchase alcohol and cigarettes) and make autonomous decisions. ALs antisocial behaviors consist mainly of minor, non-predatory offenses (e.g., public drunkenness, underage drinking, shoplifting, and vandalism) that begin in adolescence and stop around age 20 when many transition into adulthood. Moffitt's (1993) maturity gap thesis argues that as ALs enter young adulthood they are assimilated into the adult social world through an increase in adult statuses. Because of breaching the "maturity gap," delinquency for ALs declines, barring any "snares" such as an unwanted pregnancy or involvement in the juvenile justice system that may cause continued involvement in delinquency (Moffitt, 1993, p. 684).

Conversely, life course persistent offenders commit more serious crimes and begin offending at an earlier age. They participate in both minor and serious forms of delinquency as adolescents, and continue to commit violent crimes as adults (Moffitt, 1993). LCP offenders are approximately 5 percent of offenders and account for the bulk of adult offenses (Moffitt et al., 2001). Antisocial behaviors of LCPs as young children are aggravated by neuropsychological deficits and social environments characterized by instability, poverty, inadequate [harsh] parenting, and weak or disrupted social bonds (Moffitt et al., 2001). As LCPs age, relationships outside the family (such as relationships with peers and teachers) are molded by their experiences in early childhood. Throughout the first 20 years of life there is a cumulative effect of the negative transactions between the individual and his or her environment. These accumulated transactions result in a disordered personality characterized by physical aggressiveness and antisocial behaviors that continue through midlife (Moffitt, 1993; Moffitt et al., 2001).

Most adolescents commit some type of delinquency, whether as ALs or LCP offenders (Boutwell & Beaver, 2008). However, it is important to note that Moffitt also identified a third group, abstainers, who do not engage in delinquent offending at any level. Moffitt (1993) identified 3 reasons why abstainers refrain from participation in delinquency. First, some adolescents do not experience the "maturity gap" and lack the motivation for experimenting with crime. For example, youths who experience puberty later may have a shorter gap between biological and social maturation. Second, abstainers may lack opportunities for exposure to delinquent peers. Third, adolescent abstainers may have personality characteristics that make them undesirable to other youths or prevent them from seeking entry into delinquent peer groups (Moffitt, 1993).

The arrested adolescent offender is, in essence, an older version, previously unidentified, of the adolescent limited offender who has failed to make successful on-time transitions to adult roles. He or she has the same background characteristics and offending patterns as the adolescent limited offender. However, unlike Moffitt's AL, the arrested adolescent does not desist as quickly because of failure to enter adult social roles.

Based on the research findings of Arnett and others, I define the *arrested adolescent offender* as an adult between the ages of 18 and 25 who continues to commit low-level, petty offenses (e.g., theft, drug use, vandalism, disorderly conduct) at a high rate (comparable to that of ALs) (Salvatore & Welsh, 2008, Salvatore & Welsh, 2009). The arrested adolescent offender engages in crime and deviance because of failure to breach the maturity gap (Moffitt, 1993) and achieve adult status, as symbolized by reaching the turning points of marriage, stable employment, and completion of higher education. Like most offenders, arrested adolescent offenders will desist as they adopt adult roles and assimilate into conventional society. The arrested adolescent offender would most likely have offended as an adolescent limited offender during adolescence. It is also possible that abstainers may start offending during emerging adulthood as arrested adolescent offenders due to the failure to reach turning points and establish social bonds.

The arrested adolescent offender is similar to the adolescent limited offender in that his or her background shows no neuropsychological deficiencies such as ADHD, and offending is the result of dysphoria and the lack of social bonds (e.g., having a spouse, being a parent) (see Table 1). Unlike the adolescent limited offender, the arrested adolescent offender has chronologically aged out of adolescence but has failed to breach the maturity gap. Stuck in the emergent adulthood stage of the life course, the arrested adolescent offender has not transitioned to adult roles and continues to engage in low-level offenses typical of ALs. It should be noted that what separates LCP offenders from ALs and AAOs is their (LCP) involvement in serious crimes such as burglary and rape. During the emergent adulthood stage of the life course, LCPs will continue to offend at higher rates than AAOs and commit violent and predatory crimes (Moffitt et al., 2001).

Support for the idea that emerging adulthood influences offending can be found in Moffitt, Caspi, Harrington, & Milne (2002). Using a more recent wave of data from the Dunedin study, researchers found that at age 26 some of the adolescent limited offenders identified earlier in the study had many legal and personal problems, including mental health problems, property offenses, financial problems, and substance dependency. Moffitt discusses how members of the Dunedin cohort may still be experiencing many of these problems in their early 20's because of a "new developmental stage called *emerging adulthood*" (p. 200), concluding that emerging adulthood may have influenced the offending patterns of the Dunedin sample as they matured, as well other young people born after 1970.

Further, recent research (Steinberg, 2005) now suggests that brain development (e.g., nerve mylinization) continues through the twenties. This factor may add another challenge for those in emerging adulthood, as they may not yet have completed their cognitive or social development. It is beyond the scope of this study to examine the impact of brain development on those in emergent adulthood. It is possible that continuing brain development, accompanied by the stressful and confusing stage of emerging adulthood, may contribute to increased crime and delinquency.

The theoretical context presented above serves as a starting point for addressing the three goals of this study: (1) exploring the age and period effects caused by emerging adulthood by identifying the arrested adolescent offender; (2) examining characteristics of the arrested adolescent offender based on previous theory and research; and, (3) identifying how arrested adolescence modifies offending trajectories identified in the life course literature.

AGE, PERIOD, AND COHORT (APC) EFFECTS

Researchers typically classify influences that alter behaviors over time as age effects, period effects, or cohort effects (Taylor, 1994). O'Malley et al. (1984) defined *age effects* as "developmental or maturational changes which show up consistently" (p. 682). Age effects are limited to a specific age group, and refer to both physiological processes (e.g., puberty) and social processes (e.g., the beginning of schooling) (Fabio, Loeber, Balasubramani, Roth, Fu, & Farrington, 2006). Age effects also include the accumulation of social experiences and the role of status or role changes (Yang & Land, 2007).

Period effects refer to changes that occur with time across all age groups because of specific factors occurring during a specific time (O'Malley et al., 1984). These changes influence the likelihood that individuals will participate in certain behaviors or have certain attitudes (Taylor, 1994). Period effects reflect the influence of historical events on all groups during a specific time period (Menard, 1992). All groups are affected at the same time, usually as the result of societal changes (e.g., economic, cultural) (Yang & Land, 2007). An important aspect of period effects discussed by Fabio et al. (2006) is that they are short term and usually recede once the social factor dissipates. The researchers also refer to the economy as an example of a period effect; when the economy is weak, the availability of legal jobs is diminished and the risk of performing illicit jobs increases. Once the economy rebounds, job availability increases and the risk of partaking in the illicit economy decreases.

Cohort effects refer to sustained differences in birth cohorts that persist over the life course (Fabio et al., 2006). In other words, cohort effects are the result of being a member of a specific group or cohort that affects the member's attitudes and behaviors (Taylor, 1994). For example, Donohue & Levitt (2001) and Levitt & Dubner (2005) theorized that legalized abortion resulted in fewer births of undesired children who are more crime prone. Thus, according to Donohue & Levitt (2001) and Levitt & Dubner (2005), a cohort born after the legalization of abortion would be expected to have fewer individuals who are likely to commit crime.

Examining the independent and interactive effects of age, historical period, and cohort membership on a dependent variable (e.g., rate of offending) would be an ideal approach for examining how societal changes are altering offending patterns over time. However, there is considerable debate about whether this is possible. Mason, Mason, Winsborough, & Poole (1973) argued that any attempt to simultaneously estimate age, period, and cohort effects would be problematic: "Unless two of these three variables are viewed as indexing identical unmeasured causal factors, any analysis which makes estimates for only two of the three variables is subject to spurious results" (p. 242). Any analysis that simultaneously incorporates age, period, and cohort effects is difficult because all three effects are linearly dependent on one another (Mason et al., 1973). Blalock (1966) referred to this dilemma as the identification problem. Blalock (1966) argued the identification problem occurs because there are too many unknowns for a solution. Identification is possible in one-way causal situations by making assumptions about the error terms, but these are often unrealistic. Blalock (1966) stated that, "Even this procedure breaks down when exact mathematical relationships are assumed among some of the variables, as is the case where status inconsistency (or social mobility) is taken as a difference between two statuses" (p. 52). In other words, even though age, period, and cohort effects are different conceptually they are operationally dependent and confounded with one another (Baltes, 1968). O'Malley, Bachman, & Johnston (1984) have argued in this regard that any statistical model that attempts to estimate age, period, and cohort effects is unidentifiable, and it is not possible to model the linear effects of all three factors simultaneously.

In order to avoid this identification problem, it has been suggested that one or more of the three APC effects be excluded in any single study (Baltes, 1968). Yang (2008) discussed how the APC identification problem may not occur in cross sectional studies. The identification problem is typically an issue with aggregate data (often limited to age and period measured in one-or-five year intervals) that create the linear dependency issue (Yang, 2008). Yang states that using a repeated cross sectional survey we can, "use different temporal groupings for the age, period, and cohort variables to break the linear dependency" (p. 210). It should be noted that while Yang's (2008) suggestion offers a possible solution to the identification problem, this type of data is rarely available in longitudinal studies that measure delinquent and criminal behavior. In sum, the identification problem is a challenge for any analysis incorporating APC effects. In order to address this issue, data analysis needs to be tailored to the specific APC effect(s) the study seeks to examine (Baltes, 1968; O'Brien, 2000; Yang, 2008),

Palmore (1978) stated that there are essential differences to each of the APC effects that need to be considered when conducting analyses. Age effects are longitudinal in nature. In this study age effects are represented by the accumulation of social experiences and role changes (e.g., getting married, having children). Period effects are also longitudinal in nature, and are reflected in this study as social and economic changes (Yang, 2008) that have occurred since 1960. A cohort effect can be used to compare different groups of people over the life course (Yang, 2008), which would not be applicable for a study examining longitudinal data using a single cohort. This study requires longitudinal data examining data in a cohort over time in order to explore the influence of emerging adulthood on offending. Palmore (1978) identified both age and period effects as occurring within longitudinal data, supporting the examination of age and period effects for this study. Taylor (1994) has noted that a longitudinal panel survey (such as the Add Health data used for this study) featuring a cohort whose members are different ages can adequately separate age and period effects. Add Health is limited to one cohort and will prevent the inclusion of cohort effects in this study. Further, none of the hypotheses of this study are related to cohort effects.

Based on the conceptual model of arrested adolescence and the justifications discussed above, this study focuses exclusively on age and period effects by examining how changes brought about by emerging adulthood have influenced the offending patterns of young adults. Specifically, age effects are represented by examining transitions to age-related social roles (e.g., marriage, having children). Period effects are represented by the delay in social transitions (e.g., economic and cultural) examined in this study. Implementing recommendations proposed by prior researchers (viz., Baltes, 1968; O'Brien, 2000; Taylor, 1994; Yang, 2008) should effectively minimize the identification problem and successfully analyze age and period effects.

PRIOR CRIMINOLOGICAL STUDIES USING ADD HEALTH DATA

The use of longitudinal panel survey data such as the Add Health data provides two advantages: (1) it can address APC concerns as discussed above; and (2) it provides good measures of theoretical constructs suggested by Arnett's theory of emerging adulthood.

Add Health data have been used extensively in both the social and medical sciences. Topics examined by Add Health researchers include: intergenerational religious dynamics and adolescent delinquency (Pearce & Haynie, 2004), the role of residential mobility and deviant behaviors (Haynie , South, & Bose, 2006a; Haynie, South, & Bose, 2006b, South & Haynie, 2004), pubertal development and victimization and delinquency (Haynie & Piquero, 2006; Haynie, 2003), the role of relationships during adolescence and offending (Armour & Haynie, 2007, Haynie, 2002, Haynie, Giordano, Manning, & Longmore, 2005, Haynie & McHugh, 2003, Haynie & Osgood, 2005, Haynie & Payne, 2006, Haynie, Silver, & Teasdale, 2006), and the relationships between race, the economic maturity gap, and offending in young adulthood (Haynie, Weiss, & Piquero, 2008). This latter study is of particular interest to this study because of its theoretical and methodological contributions.

Haynie, Weiss, and Piquero (2008) examined whether economic and employment factors could explain group-based (e.g., race) differences and changes in offending over time among adolescents. This research question is similar to that of the present study which seeks to examine whether delayed turning points explain group-based differences (i.e., the subgroups identified by Moffitt) and changes in the period of active offending over time. Although Haynie et al. (2008) used information from all 3 waves to construct their dependent variables, their analyses were cross sectional rather than longitudinal (i.e., they did not analyze data at all 3 waves simultaneously).

Four dependent variables were used in the study: (1) a global measure of self- reported criminal involvement at wave 3; (2) a dichotomous measure of violence involvement at wave 3; (3) a dichotomous measure of persistence coded 1 for those who reported participation in criminal activities at waves 1 and 2 (and no involvement at wave 3); and, (4) a measure of violence persistence (coded 1 if respondents reported violent behavior at waves 1 and 2 and coded as 0 if they only reported violent behavior at wave 2). Independent variables included race (3 mutually exclusive categories): African American, other race/ethnicity, and White.

Measures of economic and employment prospects were derived from wave 3 responses of current job assessment (working full or part time, or unemployed; occupation-low or high skill) and economic well-being (owning a house, condo, or motor home; having a checking account or credit card; having had any utilities shut off for non-payment). Control variables included gender, family structure (measured using a dichotomous variable indicating whether the respondent resided in a 2 parent family (=1) or other family type (=0) during the wave 1 survey. Family socioeconomic status was taken from items on the parent's questionnaire at wave 1 that measured mother's and father's occupation and education. Other controls included respondents' current (measured at wave 3) living situations including marital status (1=yes, 0=no), whether the respondent was currently receiving welfare (1=yes, 0=no), and whether the respondent was currently in school full or part time (1=yes, 0=no).

Four key findings emerged from the analyses. First, when examining criminal offending generally, blacks were more likely than whites to offend. At the same time, and consistent with Moffitt and Elliott, respectively, economic and employment prospects mediated the effects of race on criminal offending and rendered the variable insignificant. Second, when examining persistence in criminal offending race by itself was not significant, suggesting that once involved in offending, race alone was no longer a predictive factor. This result was consistent with two previous studies on the correlates of crime participation and persistence, both of which found significant race effects for initial participation but not for continued offending (Blumstein et al., 1986; Piquero et al., 2003). Several economic and employment variables were nevertheless related to persistence in offending. Third, when exploring the correlates of violent offending, Haynie et al. found that Blacks were over-represented in self-reported violence. However, once economic and employment prospects were controlled in the model, the race gap in violence was diminished (and rendered non-significant) (p. 609). Last, when they explored the correlates of persistence in violence, the researchers (as Elliott previously had) found that blacks were more likely than whites to persist in violence (p. 611). However, when controlling for economic and employment prospects, the race effect was reduced to non-significance, a finding consistent with Moffitt's hypothesis that the economic maturity gap accounts for race differences in violent behavior among young adult criminals.

The application of techniques used by Haynie et al. (2008) to measure key theoretical constructs (e.g., offender subgroups such as LCP and AL, severity and type of offending) and analyze Add Health data (e.g., using a series of count regression models) are discussed further in the Methods section (Ch. 3).

STATEMENT OF RESEARCH QUESTION AND KEY HYPOTHESES

This study explores how trajectories of low-level offenders identified by prior researchers in the area of life course criminology as adolescent limited offenders are prolonged when one enters emerging adulthood. If adolescence is play, then emerging adulthood will delay many traditional turning points (e.g., marriage, having children, attaining full-time employment) that often serve to increase social bonds and inhibit low level offending. The main research prediction of this study is as follows: Emerging adulthood has extended the period of active offending for some adolescent limited offenders by delaying traditional turning points that encourage low-level offenders to decrease participation in crime and deviance.

The hypotheses listed below represent measures of turning points and social bonds that the men in Laub and Sampson's (2003) sample identified as factors that influenced their desistance. In addition, many of these indicators have been examined in prior research examining crime and deviance during emerging adulthood (Chasin, Pitts, & Prost, 2002; Rohrbach, Sussmann, Dent, & Sun, 2005; Tucker, Ellickson, Orlando, Martino, & Klein, 2005; White, Labouvie, & Papadaratsakis, 2005).

The following is a list of individual hypotheses related to this core prediction: (see Table 1 for sample ages at each wave)

1   Emerging adults who do not marry will have a greater likelihood of continued involvement in low-level offending as AAOs in wave 3 relative to those emerging adults who marry.

2   Emerging adults who delay having children at wave 3 will be more likely to continue offending as AAOs at wave 3 compared to those who have children.

3   Emerging adults who work more hours at wave 3 will be less likely to engage in crime and delinquency as AAOs at wave 3 compared to those who work fewer hours.

4   Emerging adults who are actively serving in the military at wave 3 will be less likely to commit low-level offenses as AAOs at wave 3 compared to those not serving in the military.

5   Emerging adults who have higher levels of education at wave 3 will offend at lower rates at wave 3 compared to those with lower levels of education.

6   Emerging adults who have higher levels of job satisfaction at wave 3 will participate in lower levels of crime at wave 3.

7   Emerging adults who have higher levels of religious participation at wave 3 will be less likely to continue to offend during emerging adulthood when compared with those who have lower participation in religious services at wave 3.

8   Emerging adults who have stronger social bonds to parents at wave 3 will have lower rates of criminal offending as AAOs at wave 3 compared to those who have weaker parental bonds.

9   Participants who score higher on economic insatiability at wave 3 will be more likely to offend as AAOs relative to those who score lower on economic instability.

10 Participants who score lower on property owned at wave 3 will be more likely to offend as AAOs compared to those who score higher.

11 Analyses will also examine whether any abstainers (at waves 1 and 2) committed offenses at wave 3. I predict that there may be a small percentage of abstainers at waves 1 and 2 that may commit low-level (AAO) offenses at wave 3. Moffitt et al. (2002) found that a small percentage of abstainers in adolescence committed low-level offenses (e.g., rule violations, property offenses, and drug offenses) in their 20s. Examining abstainers will allow me to study whether Moffitt et al.'s (2002) findings are applicable to this sample.

12 I predict that the same turning points and social bonds examined in hypotheses 1 though 10 will predict offending for "late bloomers" identified in hypothesis 11. Moffitt et al. (2002) found that a small percentage of individuals experience the onset of delinquency post-puberty. Here I will be able to examine those individuals and explore the influence emerging adulthood has on their offending patterns.

The focus of this study is on how indicators of arrested adolescence are influencing offending over time. At each level of analysis, the above hypotheses will also be tested for LCP offenders. I postulate that these AAO indicators will not have any influence on LCP offending, as LCPs offending is not rooted in social maturation. However, by providing examinations of the influence of arrested adolescence on life course persistent offenders, this study may help clarify the role (or lack of) emerging adulthood with LCPs.

CHAPTER 3

Examination of The Arrested Adolescent Offender

This chapter provides an overview of the dataset used for this study, a detailed description of the variables being examined, and the analytical plan developed to test hypotheses set forth in the proceeding chapters

DESIGN AND SAMPLING STRUCTURE OF THE ADD HEALTH DATA

Data from the National Longitudinal Study of Adolescent Health (Add Health) is utilized for this study. The Add Health is a longitudinal panel survey of adolescents and young adults who were enrolled from 7th through 12th grades during the 1994-1995 academic year (Harris et al., 2003). The Add Health project currently consists of three waves of data featuring multiple data components, including results from in school surveys, in-home surveys, and parent interviews. The purpose of the Add Health study was to create a nationally representative sample of adolescent youth from which data could be collected to measure the impact of various social factors on adolescent health and general well-being in the United States. These factors included the effects of peers, family, education, religion, and community on adolescent health (Harris et al., 2003). The study was mandated by the U.S. Congress in the NIH Revitalization Act of 1993 and has been used extensively to study delinquency (see, for example, Felson & Haynie, 2002; Haynie, 2002; Haynie, 2003; Haynie, Giordana, Manning, & Longmore, 2005; Haynie, Petts, Maimon, & Piquero, 2008; Pierce & Haynie, 2004).

The data used for this study come from the public use survey for all three waves of the Add Health data that are publicly available from the Interuniversity Consortium for Political and Social Research (ICPSR).

The Add Health study collected multiple panels of data over three waves. The in-home portion of the survey is utilized for this study because it includes questions regarding health status, peer networks, crime and delinquency, sexual and romantic relationships, and education and employment aspirations.

The Add Health study was chosen for several reasons. First, the survey provides comprehensive information on one of the most recent cohorts expected to experience emergent adulthood. Next, the sample size of 6,500 cases (unweighted) is large enough to conduct sophisticated statistical analyses (Stevens, 1996) and includes sampling weights that allow the information to be applied to the national population (Chantala & Tabor, 1999). These data also contain various demographic variables as well as measures of employment, education, social bonds to friends and family (e.g., marital status, having children, closeness of relationship to parents and sibling), and military service. The survey data also capture information on a diverse range of delinquent and criminal activity (e.g., stealing, sexual assault, shoplifting, vandalism), with respondents reporting involvement in these acts on a scale ranging from 0 (never) to 3 (5 or more times). Collecting such data from a broadly representative sample has been encouraged by researchers who have stated that to effectively detect correlates of persistent crime or psychopathology it is best to utilize representative population samples rather than solely delinquent samples (Moffitt, 1993).

Data from wave 1 of the in-home interviews were collected between April and December 1995. Respondents completed the surveys using laptop computers to ensure confidentiality and, given that wave 1 respondents ranged from ages 11 through 21 (mean = 16), screening questions were asked to ensure the age appropriateness of the survey. Among the topics included at wave 1 were employment experience, educational aspirations and expectations, substance use, delinquent/criminal activities, the ordering of events leading to romantic and sexual partnerships, peer networks, and family composition and relationships (Udry, 1998). Additional questions dealing with the co-occurrence of risk behaviors were posed to respondents who had indicated that they had engaged in such behaviors separately (e.g., committing a crime while using drugs) (Udry, 1998).

Wave 2 data were collected approximately one year later, between April and August of 1996 when members of the sample were aged 12 through 22 (mean = 17) (Harris et al., 2003). Data collections at this wave were the same as those implemented at wave 1, except that several questions related to health and weight were added (Udry, 1998). The core sample consisted of all respondents to the Wave 1 in-home interview (N = 4834) (Udry, 1998).

Wave 3 data were collected between August 2001 and April 2002 when respondents were between the ages of 18 and 28 (mean = 22) (Udry, 2003). Because many of the respondents were now young adults, wave 3 was designed to gather data that could assist researchers in studying the transitions between adolescence and young adulthood (Udry, 2003). As a result, some questions were removed from the survey and more age-appropriate questions dealing with topics such as military service were added (Udry, 2003, p. 3).

Data collection procedures for wave 3 consisted of follow-up interviews of the original Wave 1 participants who were located by field interviewers, with interviews being conducted in all 50 states (Udry, 2003, p.3). Respondents who were out of the county or enlisted in the Armed Forces and deployed out of the county were not included; those who were on active duty service in the U.S. were included (Udry, 2003). While some researchers have suggested that this fact brings into question the utility of examining military service (Stevens, 1996), others have argued that it is theoretically justified to include this variable in the analyses to help clarify how military service acts (or fails to act) as a turning point for recent cohorts (see Laub & Sampson, 2003; Sampson & Laub, 1993; Wright, Carter, & Cullen, 2005). The wave 3 public use in-home sample provides data from 4,882 respondents (Udry, 2003).

The advantages of the Add Health data are numerous and include the ability to analyze a recent cohort of emerging adults with a large, representative sample size across a variety of racial/ethnic and socio-economic groups. This is beneficial because it will allow the findings to be as generalizable as possible. The Add Health study has been used by numerous researchers to examine relationships between social and biological maturation and offending (e.g., Boutwell & Beaver, 2008; Beaver, DeLisi, Vaughn, & Wright, 2008; Guo, et al., 2008). This study, however, will be the first to use Add Health data specifically to study how emerging adulthood influences offending according to Arnett's (2005) theory.

LIMITATIONS OF ADD HEALTH

The National Longitudinal Study of Adolescent Health has some of the same limitations as similar studies (e.g., the National Youth Survey). Foremost among them is the problem of missing data due to non-response. Although the overall response rate at wave 3 of data collection was 75.6%, researchers on the Add Health project have concluded that the wave 1 sample is adequately represented at wave 3 (Chanrala, Kalsbeek, & Andraca, 1999). The missing values analyses will be discussed under the "Analyses" subsection later in this chapter.

These data are limited to three waves and only wave 3 provides information during emerging adulthood. This limits the ability of this study to examine the long term influence of emerging adulthood on offending. Further, this restricts multivariate analysis to wave 3 only. Cross sectional analysis will allow the study to examine whether there is a relationship between the independent variables, but not if a particular independent variable causes offending. For example, conducting cross sectional analysis at wave 3 will be able to test if marital status predicts offending, but not if marital status causes offending. Further, Add Health is limited to one cohort and will prevent the inclusion of cohort effects in this study.

Other limitations present in this study include a lack of consistent use of the same questions across all three waves of data, as well as the fact that the data currently available follow subjects only up to age 28. These limitations will be addressed in greater detail in the analytic plan described below.

DEPENDENT VARIABLES

The dependent variables used for this study were selected from the crime and delinquency scale featured in the Add Health dataset at waves 1, 2, and 3. All variables used for cross sectional analysis were z-scored and scales mean summed. Using z-scores allowed for a comparison of relative values of several different variables for a case (Norusis, 2002, p. 89). All variables used for multivariable analysis were summed scales.

AL/AAO Delinquency

Based on the criteria identified by Moffitt's developmental taxonomy (Moffitt, 1993; Moffitt et al., 2001), AL and AAO offending is mainly restricted to lower level forms of crime and delinquency. As a result, a 7-item minor delinquency scale based on scales used in prior studies (viz., Barnes & Beaver, 2010; Boutwell & Beaver, 2008; Beaver et al., 2010; Haynie, Weiss, & Piquero, 2008; Pearce & Haynie, 2004), was created at wave 1 ($\alpha = 0.746$). The items on these scales consisted of low level forms of delinquency and status offenses committed during the past 12 months, including painting graffiti, damaging the property of others, shoplifting, running away from home, lying to parents about whereabouts, stealing something worth less than $50, and being loud and rowdy in public. The response categories were coded as follows: 0 = never, 1 = one or two times, 2 = three or four times, and 3 = five or more times. The seven items were subjected to principal components analysis (PCA) using SPSS version 17. The Kaiser-Meyer-Oklin[3] value was 0.742, exceeding the recommended value of .6 (Kaiser, 1970, 1974) and Bartlett's (1954) Test of Sphericity reached statistical significance, supporting the factorability of the correlation matrix.

Principal components analysis revealed the presence of two components with eigenvalues exceeding 1, explaining 41.90% and 14.37% of the variance respectively. An inspection of the scree plot revealed a clear break after the first component. As a result, it was decided to re-run the analysis, extracting only one component that explained 41.90% of the variance. One component was extracted to consolidate the variables that best represented the types of crime theorized that this group would commit. This strategy was used to create all of the dependent variable scales.

At wave 2 the same 7 items were utilized for the minor delinquency scale ($\alpha = 0.738$). The 7 items were subjected to principal components analysis (PCA). The Kaiser-Meyer-Oklin value was 0.733, and Bartlett's test of Sphericity (Bartlett, 1954) reached statistical significance, supporting the factorability of the correlation matrix. This analysis revealed the presence of two components with eigenvalues exceeding 1, explaining 41.52% and 14.52% of the variance respectively. An inspection of the scree plot revealed a clear break after

---

[3] The Kaiser-Meyer-Oklin value measures sampling adequacy, ranges from 0 to 1, .6 is considered the minimum value for factor analysis (Pallant, 2007).

the first component. It was decided to re-run the analysis extracting only one component that explained 41.52% of the variance.

At wave 3 some of the lower level forms of crime and status offenses were removed from the delinquency scale and several non-violent offenses were added. The five items comprising this scale were theoretically justified based on previously established expectations of patterns of AAO offending (e.g., Beaver et al., 2010). The crimes in the AAO offending scale (committed during the past 12 months) included damaging the property of others, stealing an item worth less than $50, buying, selling, or holding stolen property, using someone else's credit card, bank card, or automatic teller card without their permission or knowledge, and deliberately writing a bad check (α = 0.586).[4] Responses for the wave 3 variables were also coded 0 = never, 1= one or two times, 2 = three or four times, and 3 = five or more times. The five items were subjected to principal components analysis, which yielded a Kaiser-Meyer-Oklin value of 0.685 that was significant using Bartlett's test of Sphericity. The analysis revealed the presence of one component with an eigenvalue exceeding 1, explaining 38.94% of the variance.

The mean summed scales for all three waves were compiled so that higher values reflected greater levels of participation in non-violent forms of delinquency/crime. Descriptive statistics for all scales are presented in Table 2 and complete listings of all the items that make up the scales are included in Appendix A.

---

[4] Coefficient alpha is one of the most commonly used measures of reliability. Not only is it influenced by the average correlation among items (internal consistency), but also by the number of items in the scale (Nunnally, 1978). As a result, it may be difficult to obtain a high alpha, especially in longitudinal data where variables present at one wave may not be present at the next. Psychometricians (e.g. Cronbach, 1951; 1970) have warned of this limitation, but it is often overlooked (Welsh, 2001). Further, alpha coefficients in the 0.40 - 0.50 range have generally been considered acceptable for etiological research (Thorndike, 1971).

Table 2. *Descriptive Statistics for Dependent Variables*

Dependent Variables	N	Mean	SD
Cross – Sectional Z scored (Bivariate Analysis)			
Wave 1			
Adolescent Limited Offending	6462	-.0002	0.639
Life Course Persistent Offending	6457	.138	0.286
Adolescent Limited Drug Use	6464	.001	0.787
Life Course Persistent Drug Use	6420	.0028	0.776
Wave 2			
Adolescent Limited Offending	4808	.0006	0.637
Life Course Persistent Offending	4808	.0004	0.627
Adolescent Limited Drug Use	4809	.0014	0.780
Life Course Persistent Drug Use	4802	.0011	0.731
Wave 3			
Arrested Adolescent Offending	4850	.000	0.615
Life Course Persistent Offending	4852	.0029	0.595
Arrested Adolescent Drug Use	4856	-.0003	0.756
Life Course Persistent Drug Use	4815	.0005	0.882
Wave 3 Summed Scales (Multivariate Analysis)			
Arrested Adolescent Offending	4850	.344	.988
Life Course Persistent Offending	4852	.408	1.23
Arrested Adolescent Drug Use	4856	1.95	1.02
Life Course Persistent Drug Use	4815	.260	.587

*Descriptive information reported here reflects the primary data. No imputation or deletion procedures have been applied to the dependent variables.

LCP Delinquency

Moffitt (1993) stated that LCP offenders commit a variety of offenses, particularly more serious, victim-oriented and violent offenses. Additional research by Moffitt (2006) found that LCPs were more likely to commit more serious offenses than ALs. Thus, emerging adulthood should not influence serious forms of delinquency. To examine this hypothesis, serious delinquency/crime scales were created for each wave, based again on prior research (Barnes & Beaver, 2010; Boutwell & Beaver, 2008; Beaver et al., 2010).

At wave 1 the following seven items were included in the LCP scale ($\alpha = 0.711$): hurting someone bad enough that they need bandages or care from a doctor or nurse, stealing a car, stealing something worth more than \$50, burglarizing a house or building, threatening to use a weapon to get something from someone, selling marijuana or other drugs, and taking part in a fight where a group of your friends was against another group. All items were committed during the past 12 months. The seven items yielded a Kaiser-Meyer-Oklin value of 0.789 that was statistically significant using Bartlett's test of Sphericity. The analysis revealed the presence of two components with eigenvalues exceeding 1, explaining 38.32% and 14.94% of the variance, respectively. An inspection of the scree plot revealed a clear break after the first component. It was decided to re-run the analysis extracting only one that explained 38.32% of the variance.

At wave 2 some items were removed and additional ones added. Inclusion of additional serious crimes was based on the criteria of LCP offenses types outlined by Moffitt (1993). The wave 2 scale ($\alpha = 0.709$) consisted of the following seven items: stealing a car, stealing something worth more than \$50, burglarizing a house or building, threatening to use a weapon to get something from someone, selling marijuana or other drugs, taking part in a fight where a group of your friends was against another group, and being initiated into a gang (all items were committed during the past 12 months). The Kaiser-Meyer-Oklin value was 0.810, exceeding the recommend value of .6 (Kaiser, 1970, 1974) and reached statistical significance using Bartlett's test. The analysis revealed the presence of two components with eigenvalues exceeding 1, explaining 38.99% and 14.42% of the variance, respectively. An inspection of the scree plot revealed a clear break after the first component. It was decided to re-run the analysis extracting only one component that explained 39.00% of the variance.

In the wave 3 scale ($\alpha = 0.644$), several items were different due to slight changes in the survey design for wave 3. The seven items included in the wave 3 LCP crime scale included: steal something worth more than $50, burglarize a house or building, threaten to use a weapon to get something from someone, sell marijuana or other drugs, and take part in a fight where a group of your friends was against another group, use a weapon in a fight, and carry a gun to work or school during the past 12 months. The 7 items were subjected to principal components analysis, with a Kaiser-Meyer-Oklin value of 0.731, exceeding the recommend value of 0.6 (Kaiser, 1970, 1974). Bartlett's test of Sphericity reached statistical significance, supporting the factorability of the correlation matrix.

The analysis further revealed the presence of two components with eigenvalues exceeding 1, explaining 32.32% and 15.82% of the variance, respectively. As noted above, inspection of the scree plot revealed a clear break after the first component. Thus, it was decided to re-run the analysis extracting only one component that explained 32.32% of the variance.

AL/AAO Drug Use

Moffitt (1993) argued that many AL offenders would experiment with drugs and alcohol as a representation of their movement towards independence and maturity. As a result, a low-level drug use scale for each wave of data based on operationalizations was derived from other research that has used the Add Health data (e.g., Barnes & Beaver, 2010; Boutwell & Beaver, 2008; Beaver et al., 2010). The items were dichotomous (0 = no, 1 = yes) and responses were z scored and mean summed at each wave. This procedure created drug use scales in which higher scores reflect more low-level drugs used. The wave 1 ($\alpha = 0.690$) AL/low-level drugs used scale consisted of respondents' lifetime use of alcohol, cigarettes, and marijuana. The 3 items were subjected to principal components analysis, with a Kaiser-Meyer-Oklin value of 0.666 and a significant test of Sphericity, supporting the factorability of the correlation matrix. Principal components analysis revealed the presence of one component with eigenvalue exceeding 1, explaining 61.78% of the variance.

The wave 2 ($\alpha = 0.672$) AL/low-level drugs used scale measured drug use since the last interview date. The 3 items were the same as wave 1, with a Kaiser-Meyer-Oklin value of .664 and a significant test of Sphericity, supporting the factorability of the correlation matrix. Principal components analysis revealed the presence of one component with an eigenvalue exceeding 1, explaining 60.61% of the variance.

The wave 3 (α = 0.621) AAO/low-level drugs used scale measured the types of drugs used as waves 1 and 2, asking respondents if they were used since the last interview date. These 3 items were subjected to PCA, with a Kaiser-Meyer-Oklin value of 0.646 and a significant test of Sphericity, supporting the factorability of the correlation matrix. Principal components analysis revealed the presence of one component with eigenvalue exceeding 1, explaining 56.86% of the variance.

LCP Drug Use

In keeping with Moffitt's (1993) developmental taxonomy, it is expected that arrested adolescence would not be predictive of more serious forms of drugs used that would be expected of LCPs. To test this hypothesis, LCP drug use scales were created at waves 1, 2, and 3. Participants were asked questions about their use of drugs like cocaine, inhalants, and other drugs (e.g., LSD, PCP, ecstasy, mushrooms, speed, ice, heroin, and prescription pills). The dichotomous response items were z scored and mean summed at each wave. This procedure created LCP/serious drug use scales, with higher scores reflecting greater levels of LCP/serious drug use. The wave 1 scale (α = 0.635) measured lifetime use of these drugs and produced both a Kaiser-Meyer-Oklin value of .618 and a significant test of Sphericity, supporting the factorability of the correlation matrix. Principal components analysis revealed the presence of one component with eigenvalue exceeding 1, explaining 58.90% of the variance.

The wave 2 scale (α = 0.538) measured if the respondents had used any of these drugs since the last interview and were the same as those administered at wave 1. The Kaiser-Meyer-Oklin value for this scale was 0.592, with a significant test of Sphericity, supporting the factorability of the correlation matrix. Principal components analysis revealed the presence of one component with an eigenvalue exceeding 1, explaining 52.91% of the variance.

The wave 3 scale (α = 0.710) consisted of two questions measuring usage of any type of cocaine and other types of drugs (such as LSD, PCP, ecstasy, mushrooms, speed, ice, heroin, and prescription pills) since 1995. These items were subjected to PCA, with a Kaiser-Meyer-Oklin value of 0.500 and a significant test of sphericity, supporting the factorability of the correlation matrix. Principal components analysis revealed the presence of one component with eigenvalue exceeding 1, explaining 75.54% of the variance.

Correlations between dependent variables at each wave were checked to ensure that there were differences between each variable. As expected, the dependent variables were correlated at each wave, and were of weak to moderate strength. Correlations at wave 1 ranged from .27 to .50. The correlations between wave 2 outcomes were slightly weaker, ranging from .22 to .48. At wave 3 the strength of the correlations between the outcomes decreased, ranging from .19 to.42. These correlations assure the measuring of different phenomenon was taking place (see Appendix C for discussion of alpha inflation). Tables 3 – 5 display the correlations between the four dependent variables at each wave.

Table 3.   *Wave 1 Correlation between dependent variables*

	AL Offending	LCP Offending	AL Drug Use	LCP Drug Use
AL Offending	1.00	.50**	.44**	.30**
LCP Offending	.50**	1.00	.35**	.27**
AL Drug Use	.44**	.35**	1.00	.37**
LCP Drug Use	.30**	.27**	.37**	1.00

*p<.05, **p<.01

Table 4.   *Wave 2 Correlation between dependent variables*

	AL Offending	LCP Offending	AL Drug Use	LCP Drug Use
AL Offending	1.00	.48**	.39**	.22**
LCP Offending	.48**	1.00	.36**	.25**
AL Drug Use	.39**	.36**	1.00**	.33**
LCP Drug Use	.22**	.25**	.33**	1.00**

*p<.05, **p<.01

Table 5.   *Wave 3 Correlation between dependent variables*

	AAO Offending	LCP Offending	AAO Drug Use	LCP Drug Use
AAO Offending	1.00	.37**	.19**	.22**
LCP Offending	.37**	1.00	.22**	.28**
AAO Drug Use	.19**	.22**	1.00**	.42**
LCP Drug Use	.22**	.28**	.42**	1.00**

INDEPENDENT VARIABLES

To examine the effects of demographic variables, age, gender, and race are included in the models as statistical controls. Age is measured as a continuous variable. Cases that are not in the appropriate ranges (e.g., those over age of 18 at waves 1, N = 258, and over 25 at wave 3, N = 53) are removed from the sample for analysis through the use of filter variables.

As discussed earlier the relationship between age and crime is a contentious one, with some arguing that the age-crime curve is invariant, having no variation across historical period, geographic location, or other cultural factors (Gottfredson & Hirschi, 1990). The opposing viewpoint is that the age-crime curve does demonstrate variance in factors like gender and type of crime (Moffitt et al., 2001; Moffitt, 1993; Steffensmeier, Anderson, Harer, Streifel 1989; Farrington, 1986). Although this study does not seek to test the age-crime curve, I would hypothesize that if the core research question is supported this may support the latter viewpoint that the age-crime curve does demonstrate variance based on factors such as delaying traditional turning points.

Gender is coded as "0" for male and "1" for female. Gender is of interest because prior studies (e.g., Laub & Sampson, 2003) were conducted largely with male samples. Belknap (2007) argues that female criminality has been largely unexplored relative to male criminality. Including gender in this study addresses this criticism and provides an examination of the possible differences in male and female offending during emerging adulthood. Further, inclusion of gender allows this study to examine whether the turning points and social bonds that were so effective for the men in Laub and Samson's study are effective for women.

Moffitt et al. (2001) suggested that the peak of anti-social behavior in females is near the peri-puberal period because girls at this stage are most likely to affiliate with older, delinquent male peers. Based on Moffitt et al.'s (2001) findings I would hypothesize that females during emerging adulthood would be less likely than males to offend as they have "aged out" of the period where they are most likely to participate in delinquent behavior.

Race is limited to a control variable in the analyses. While compelling in scope and methodology, studies of criminality across the life course have largely overlooked the significance of race as a demographic factor explaining differential patterns of offending. This oversight has been recognized by criminologists (Piquero et al. 2002), and has been explained as a result of the limited racial diversity found in most longitudinal datasets (Laub and Sampson 2003; Piquero et al. 2007). Recent studies (Jennings et al. 2010; Maldonado-Molina et al. 2009) have begun to address this shortcoming. Maldonado-Molina et al (2009) examined trajectories of delinquency and the relationship of risk and protective factors (e.g., self-esteen, social support), between youths from the Bronx, United States and San Juan, Puerto Rico finding that the Bronx sample had higher rates of delinquency and sensation-seeking behaviors and that the level of exposure to violence influenced offender trajectories. Results from San Juan found lower rates of delinquency, but that the risk factors had largely the same effects across both samples. More recently, Jennings et al. (2010) continued examining Hispanic samples by comparing delinquent trajectories for males and females in the Bronx, United States and San Juan, Puerto Rico. They found that in both samples, despite the fact that males offended at higher rates, risk and protective factors seemed to have similar effects across genders.

However, because of the relatively low number of other racial groups (Asian, American Indian, and Hispanic) relative to Whites and Blacks, three mutually exclusive categories are used: African American, Other Race/Ethnicity, and White. Two dummy coded variables, White (1 = White; 0= all others) and Black (1=Black; 0 = all others) are included in the multivariate models at dummy coded variables (see Table 6 for demographics). Other independent variables for each wave were grouped into several categories that describe either life-course turning points (e.g., marriage) or social bonds (e.g., school attachment). Certain variables were limited to specific waves of data collection (e.g., military service) due to the addition of age appropriate questions to the Add Health survey (see Tables 6-9 for descriptive statistics). To determine whether turning points and social bonds involving marriage and family have an independent effect on crime, several measures of turning points and social bonds are entered as predictors.

Table 6. *Descriptives of Demographics Variables Wave 1-3 (Age Filtered for Appropriate Ages Only)*

	Wave 1		Wave 2		Wave 3	
	Frequency	**%**	**Frequency**	**%**	**Frequency**	**%**
Gender						
Female	2404	52.5	2404	52.5	2608	54.0
Male	2172	47.5	2172	47.5	2221	46.0
Race						
White	2917	63.7	NA	NA	2859	59.2
Black	1031	22.5	NA	NA	1113	23.0
All Others	628	13.7	NA	NA	851	17.6
Age						
	Range = 11-18		Range = 11-18		Range = 18-25	
	Mean = 16		Mean = 16		Mean = 22	
	SD = 1.46		SD = 1.46		SD = 1.76	

Table 7. *Descriptives of Independent Variables at Wave 1 (N = 4576) Ages 11-18 Only*

Variable	Min	Max	Mean	SD	% Missing
Attendance at Religious Services	0	3	1.47	0.93	13.2
Grade in School	7	12	9.03	1.40	1.4
Hours Worked Scale	0	90	18.26	22.61	2.0
Low-Self Control Scale	0	12	3.31	2.43	1.3
Parental Attachment Scale	2	20	15.60	4.64	.8
Peabody Picture Vocabulary Test	14	139	101.15	15.08	3.7
School Attachment Scale	3	15	11.23	2.57	1.4

	Frequency	Percentage			
Marital Status:					
Not Married	4428	99.2			0
Married	35	0.8			

Table 8.   *Descriptives of Independent Variables at Wave 2 (N = 4576) Ages 11-18 Only*

Variable	Min	Max	Mean	SD	% Missing
Attendance at Religious Services	0	3	3.02	1.07	14.3
Grade in School	7	13	9.96	1.41	6.6
Hours Worked Scale	0	90	24.91	26.10	.5
Low-Self Control Scale		12	3.08	2.25	6.2
Parental Attachment Scale	2	20	17.87	2.26	1.9
School Attachment Scale	3	15	11.28	2.57	6.2

	Frequency	Percentage			
Have Any Children					
No	4504	98.4			
Yes	72	1.6			
Marital Status					
Not Married	4551	99.5			0
Married	24	.5			0

Table 9. *Descriptives of Independent Variables at Wave 3 (N = 4829) Ages 18 – 25 Only*

Variable	Min	Max	Mean	SD	%Missing
Attendance at Religious Services	0	6	2.12	1.96	.9
Highest Grade Completed	6	22	13.22	1.99	.1
Hours Worked Per Week	3	90	36.80	12.48	31.5
Job Satisfaction	1	5	3.96	.91	31.5
Economic Well Being Scale	0	5	0.44	.85	.9
Parental Attachment Scale	1	10	7.15	2.43	58.6
Property Owned Scale	0	5	2.73	1.33	.1

	Frequency	Percentage			%Missing
Have Any Children Living With You					.2
No	3334	69.0			
Yes	1483	30.7			
Marital Status					0
Not Married	4028	83.4			
Married	801	16.6			
Military Service					0
No	4747	98.3			
Yes	76	1.6			

The first independent variable is marital status, which will be measured dichotomously (0 = no; 1 = yes) and is available for all three waves. Because marital status (single) is one indicator of arrested adolescence, I hypothesize a significant relationship to exist between being single and engaging in crime at waves 2 and 3. Regarding a second indicator, whether the subject *has any children* (0 = no; 1 = yes) at waves 2 and wave 3, I hypothesize that those who do have children would be less likely to commit crime as they have stronger social bonds and parental responsibilities that act to inhibit deviance by interrupting routine activities. Next, a 4-item *parental bonds* scale (wave 1 α = 0.726; wave 2 α = 0.666) based on prior studies that have used the Add Health data (Barnes & Beaver, 2010; Boutwell & Beaver, 2008; Beaver et al., 2010) was created. Items included: how close was the respondent to their mother, how close were they to their father, how much does their Mom care, and how much does their Dad care? At wave 3, only two of the parental attachment items were available (α = 0.572) namely how close did the respondent feel they were to their mother, and how close did they feel toward their father? Responses to each question were summed in additive scales with higher values reflecting greater level of parental attachment. I hypothesize that those with greater levels of parental attachment will be less likely to offend at all waves.

To examine the influence of employment on crime, I created a composite variable that combined hours worked per week in the summer and hours worked per week during the rest of the year into a measure labeled *Hours worked per week* (wave 1 α = 0.713; wave 2 α = 0.724). I hypothesize that those who work more hours per week will be less likely to have the time and opportunity to engage in criminal activities consistent with findings of prior research that found that full-time employment to act as a turning point away from criminality for most individuals (Laub & Sampson, 2001). At wave 3, *hours worked per week* (higher score = more hours worked) and *how satisfied are you with your job* (higher score = greater level of satisfaction) were used to study the influence of employment. I hypothesize that those who work more hours will have less time to participate in criminal behavior, and those with higher levels of job satisfaction will have stronger bonds to employment and will be less likely to offend at wave 3.

The lack of economic stability has been identified as a characteristic of emerging adulthood (Arnett, 2005, Cote, 2000). To examine the influence of economics, two indices gauging economic stability are included. Those in emerging adulthood have less stable employment and income; as a result, they have less stable social bonds. I hypothesize that those who score higher on the economic well-being index at wave 3 will be more likely to offend as AAOs. The first measure is of *property owned* ($\alpha = 0.54$). I hypothesize that those who are AAO offenders will be less likely to own property because of failure to reach turning points. I hypothesize that those with greater levels of property ownership have a greater stake in conformity and would be less likely to offend. This index was used in Haynie et al., (2008) and consists of whether one owns the following items: a residence (house, condominium, or mobile home), a motor vehicle (car, truck, or motorcycle), and computer. The index also includes a question on whether one has a checking account and a credit card. Responses in the property owned scaled were summed into an additive scale with higher values reflecting greater levels of ownership.

The second index is economic instability ($\alpha = 0.57$), which was also used by Haynie et al., (2008). I hypothesize that those who score higher on the measure of economic instability will be more likely to offend as AAOs, because the measure is based on responses to the following questions: "in the past 12 months was there a time when..." "...you were without telephone service because you did not have enough money to pay the bill," "...did not have enough money to pay the full amount of rent or mortgage," "... were evicted from house/apartment for not paying the rent or mortgage," "...did not pay the full amount of gas, electric, or oil company would not deliver," and "...did not see a doctor or go to the hospital because you could not pay the bill." Responses for the economic well-being scale were summed in an additive scale, with higher scores reflecting lower levels of economic stability and well-being.

The role of education will be examined using *highest grade completed* (*higher score = more education*), a variable measured at all three waves of data collection. Completing higher education has traditionally acted as a social marker of adulthood. Those who have higher levels of education typically have greater levels of social capital, earn higher salaries, and are less likely to engage in crime (Cote, 2000).

In addition, *attachment to education* was measured using a scale based on prior studies (Barnes & Beaver, 2010; Boutwell & Beaver, 2008; Beaver et al., 2010). At waves 1 ($\alpha = 0.779$) and 2 ($\alpha = 0.786$), this scale consisted of three variables: how close did the respondent feel to people at school, how much did they feel part of their school, and how happy were they at their school? Prior research posited that greater levels of attachment to education can inhibit delinquency (Hirschi, 1969; Guo et al., 2008). Responses to each question were summed in additive scales with higher values reflecting greater levels of school attachment. The variables that make up the waves 1 and 2 educational attachment scales were not included at wave 3 and are not included in the wave 3 analysis.

To find out whether military service has an independent effect on crime, a variable available at wave 3 only that measures military service (0 = no; 1 = yes) is included. Prior research has found that military service acted as a turning point away from crime for previous generations, and military service has often been identified as a social marker of adulthood (Laub & Sampson, 2001; Okimoto & Stegall, 1987).

To study the influence of neuropsychological functioning on deviant and criminal behavior a measure of verbal abilities, the Peabody Picture Vocabulary Test (PPVT), is examined at Wave 1. Prior researchers who have used Add Health data used the PPVT as an indicator of verbal skills and receptive vocabulary (Beaver et al., 2010). Quattorocchi & Golden (1983) found that measures of verbal skills correlate with neuropsychological functioning; thus, the PPVT is scored so that higher values reflect stronger verbal abilities. Moffitt (1993) and Moffitt et al. (2001) have found that those with higher levels of verbal functioning are less likely to offend as LCPs. I hypothesize that those with lower scores on the PPVT will have higher levels of offending at each wave on the LCP offending scales.

Pratt & Cullen (2000) observed that low-self-control is one of the most consistent predictors of delinquent behavior. Self-control has been studied in prior studies analyzing Add Health data (Beaver, 2008; Beaver et al., 2010; Wright, Beaver, Delisi, & Vaugh, 2008). In this research, *Low self-control* will be measured using scales at wave 1 (α = 0.679) and wave 2 (α = 0.653) (low self-control variables were not available at wave 3) and will be based on scales used in prior studies (Beaver, 2008; Beaver et al., 2008) that consist of three questions: did respondents have trouble getting along with their teachers, did respondents have trouble completing their homework, and did respondents have trouble paying attention.

The final variable that is examined is that of *attendance at religious services* (*higher score = more participation*), a measure which is available at all three waves. Previous researchers have argued that emerging adults are less likely to engage in religious services

(Arnett, 1998), and that religious participation acts to inhibit deviance (Laub & Sampson, 2001).

In sum, the independent variables discussed allow this study to explore the influence of emerging adulthood on offending (see Table 10 for summary of independent variables at each wave). Age effects will be studied by including age in each analysis, thus allowing an examination of how developmental processes (e.g., aging) may relate to offending. Period effects will be examined by including indicators of social bonds (e.g., parental attachment) and turning points (e.g., having children, being married) that allow the researcher to address how emerging adulthood has influenced offending.

Table 10. *Summary of Independent and Demographic Variables Availability Across Waves 1-3*

Variable	Wave 1	Wave 2	Wave 3
Age	Yes	Yes	Yes
Gender	Yes	Yes	Yes
Race	Yes	No	Yes
Attendance at Religious Services	Yes	Yes	Yes
Grade in School	Yes	Yes	No
Economic Well-Being	No	No	Yes
Have Any Children	No	Yes	Yes
Highest Grade Completed	No	No	Yes
Hours Worked Scale	Yes	Yes	Yes
Job Satisfaction	No	No	Yes
Low-Self Control Scale	Yes	Yes	No
Marital Status	Yes	Yes	Yes
Military Service	No	No	Yes
Parental Attachment Scale	Yes	Yes	Yes
Peabody Picture Vocabulary Test	Yes	No	No
Property Owned	No	No	Yes
School Attachment Scale	Yes	Yes	No

ANALYSES

The following section details the analytic plan for this study. Recall the following hypotheses presented in Chapter 1:

1. Emerging adults who do not marry will have a greater likelihood of continued involvement in low-level offending as AAOs in wave 3 relative to those emerging adults who marry.[5]

2. Emerging adults who delay having children at wave 3 will be more likely to continue offending as AAOs at wave 3 compared to those who have children.

3. Emerging adults who work more hours at wave 3 will be less likely to engage in crime and delinquency as AAOs at wave 3 compared to those who work fewer hours.

4. Emerging adults who are actively serving in the military at wave 3 will be less likely to commit low-level offenses as AAOs at wave 3 compared to those not serving in the military.

5. Emerging adults who have higher levels of education at wave 3 will offend at lower rates at wave 3 compared to those with lower levels of education.

6. Emerging adults who have higher levels of job satisfaction at wave 3 will participate in lower levels of crime at wave 3.

7. Emerging adults who have higher levels of religious participation at wave 3 will be less likely to continue to offend during emerging adulthood when compared with those who have lower participation in religious services at wave 3.

8. Emerging adults who have stronger social bonds to parents at wave 3 will have lower rates of criminal offending as AAOs at wave 3 compared to those who have weaker parental bonds.

9. Participants who score higher on economic insatiability at wave 3 will be more likely to offend as AAOs relative to those who score lower on economic instability.

---

[5] At wave 3 I will limit the sample to those married after the wave 2 data was collected to ensure that only those experiencing marriage as a turning point close to or during emerging adulthood are examined.

10   Participants who score lower on property owned at wave 3 will be more likely to offend as AAOs compared to those who score higher.

11   Analyses will also examine whether any abstainers (at waves 1 and 2) committed offenses at wave 3. I predict that there may be a small percentage of abstainers at waves 1 and 2 that may commit low-level (AAO) offenses at wave 3. Moffitt et al. (2002) found that a small percentage of abstainers in adolescence committed low-level offenses (e.g., rule violations, property offenses, and drug offenses) in their 20s. Examining abstainers will allow me to study whether Moffitt et al.'s (2002) findings are applicable to this sample.

12   I predict that the same turning points and social bonds examined in hypotheses 1 though 10 will predict offending for "late bloomers" identified in hypothesis 11. Moffitt et al. (2002) found that a small percentage of individuals experience the onset of delinquency post-puberty. Here I will be able to examine those individuals and explore the influence emerging adulthood has on their offending patterns.

The focus of this research is to study the role of delayed turning points during emerging adulthood. However, the Add Health data offers rich information on the earlier stages of the life course. I begin the analysis by presenting the results of exploratory correlational analyses conducted at waves 1 and 2 measuring turning points and social bonds. This is not the ultimate goal of the study, but will provide a foundation to explore the changing role of these indicators as participants' age. Waves 1 and 2 are focused primarily on adolescence, and hence do not provide information on the sample during emerging adulthood. The results of these analyses are discussed and presented in tables (see Appendix C).[6]

Various types of analyses have been performed using Add Health data. Many studies use negative binomial regression to address the methodological problems presented by the non-normally distributed nature of the outcome variables (e.g., Armour & Haynie, 2007; Haynie, 2002; Haynie & Piquero, 2006; Haynie, South, & Bose, 2006; South &

---

[6]   Bivariate analyses will use procedures such as Sperarman's Rank Order correlation due to the non-parametric nature of the data.

Haynie, 2004). Negative binomimal regression is a statistical procedure that can be performed in the STATA program (StataCorp, 2006) and is used for regression analysis with overly dispersed outcome variables with distributions concentrated in the low end (in this case, 0). Studies have used both cross-sectional analyses (e.g., negative binomial regression) (Haynie & Osgood, 2005; Haynie, Giordana, Manning, & Longmore, 2005) or longitudinal analyses (e.g., a series of Poisson regression models) using multiple waves of the data (Armour & Haynie, 2006; Haynie, 2003; Haynie & Payne, 2006; Haynie, et al., 2008).

Haynie et al.'s (2008) methodology is of particular importance to this study because they provide suggestions for separating the sample into offender subgroups and for developing analytic strategies that allow early indicators of social bonds, economic status, and control variables to be used for an analysis measuring the economic maturity gap at wave 3. Thus, their work provides a potential framework by demonstrating that information from earlier waves can be utilized to conduct analyses at wave 3.

The multistage analytic strategy used by Haynie et al. (2008) started with race-based, bivariate differences in employment and economic prospects, as well as racial/ethnic differences in criminal offending in young adulthood. Next, a series of negative binomial regression models were used to examine the effects of these variables on the likelihood of criminal involvement at wave 3. Following this step, they examined the models separately by race/ethnicity in order to determine whether the role of economic and employment characteristics on criminal involvement are conditioned by race (p. 609). Next, Haynie et al. used negative binomial regression to examine the effects of race on respondents' likelihood of persisting in criminal involvement between waves 2 and 3. Again, they explored the impact of economic and employment prospects in young adulthood on criminal involvement. They then turned their focus to respondents' involvement in violent behavior using a dichotomous measure of violence followed by equations predicting persistence in violence between waves 2 and 3.

To examine whether emerging adulthood is influencing offending, AL offenders need to be distinguished from LCP offenders, as these groups were described by Moffitt (1993). A dichotomous "adolescent limited" variable was created with Add Health data by employing the three-step procedure used by Barnes and Beaver (2010). First, the wave 1 and wave 2 serious delinquency scales were merged into a single additive scale. Barnes and Beaver (2010) argued that the serious delinquency scale was more appropriate than a general delinquency scale because of Moffitt's hypothesis that LCPs would have greater levels of involvement in serious delinquency than ALs. Using serious delinquency scales allowed for a more accurate distinction between LCP and AL offenders (Barnes & Beaver, 2010). Barnes & Beaver (2010) then removed abstainers, those with a score of zero on this scale, from the sample.

The last step in Barnes and Beaver's process dichotomized the remaining sample into two groups: AL and LCP offenders. ALs were defined as respondents who scored below the 95th percentile on serious delinquency. AL offenders were assigned a value of "1." Conversely, LCP offenders were defined as respondents who scored *higher* than the 95th percentile. LCP offenders were assigned a value of "0." I used a multi-stage process based on Barnes and Beaver's for separating the sample into groups at each wave. At wave 1 the serious delinquency items were merged into one scale. ALs were defined as respondents who scored below the 95th percentile on serious delinquency; LCPs were defined as the upper 5 percentile, and abstainers as those with a score of "0." At waves 2, the serious delinquency scales for both waves 1 and 2 were merged and the same procedure utilized to separate the groups at wave 1 was employed.

At wave 3 an amended two–step procedure was used. The first step used only the serious crime scale from wave 3 of the data. This adjustment was made because there is approximately 5 years between waves 2 and 3, including data from the earlier waves in the taxonomy at wave 3 may have artificially inflated the group sizes. Next, AAOs were defined as respondents who scored below the 95th percentile on serious delinquency; abstainers as those with a score of "0"; LCPs were those in the upper 5 percentile of the LCP offending scale. The next step was to identify AL offenders who continue to offend at wave 3 as "arrested adolescent offenders." The analyses examining "persisters" was accomplished using the strategy employed by Haynie et al. (2008); they created two measures of persistence in criminal offending using the self-reported delinquency and crime information from waves 2 and 3 (see Table 11).

It should be noted that the distributions of the offender groups change from wave to wave, with AL and LCPs having the most members in each group at wave 2. This was expected as members of both groups would be at their peak ages of offending at wave 2 and group membership would increase significantly for AL offenders (from

32.2% of the sample at wave 1 to 41.6% of the sample at wave 2, and about a 1% increase from 5.1% of the sample at wave 1 to 6.6% of the sample at wave 2 for LCPs. As the sample aged, it was expected that there would be a significant drop in low level offenders at wave 3 (AAOs are approximately 11% of the sample at wave 3), but the percent of LCPs in the sample would be fairly consistent. As Moffitt (1993) discussed, the turning points and social bonds that would prompt most ALs to desist would not have the same influence on LCPs.

Table 11. *Offender Typologies Waves 1-3*

Abstainers		Adolescent Limited Offenders		Life Course Persistent Offenders		Arrested Adolescent Offender	
Wave 1							
Frequency	Percent	Frequency	Percent	Frequency	Percent	Frequency	Percent
2816	61.5	1475	32.2	234	5.1	NA	NA
Wave 2							
Frequency	Percent	Frequency	Percent	Frequency	Percent	Frequency	Percent
2365	51.7	1902	41.6	301	6.6	NA	NA
Wave 3							
Frequency	Percent	Frequency	Percent	Frequency	Percent	Frequency	Percent
3976	82.3	NA	NA	306	6.3	518	10.7

As discussed previously, Add Health was designed as a cluster sample with unequal probability and the respondents nested within schools. Chantala & Tabor (1999) stated that the sample design of Add Health adds a level of complexity to analysis of the data, and that failure to account for the design may result in analyses with biased parameter estimates and incorrect variance estimates. To account for this design, special software (such as STATA) has been designed to analyze data from complex surveys such as Add Health and should be used when running multivariate analysis (Chantala & Tabor, 1999). STATA can correct for design effects and unequal probability of outcome, thus allowing the estimates and standard errors to be unbiased (Chantala & Tabor, 1999). STATA provides another benefit over other statistical packages (such as SPSS or SAS) in that it has a regression procedure, negative binomial regression, designed for data where the distribution of the dependent variables are highly skewed, with a large proportion of participants reporting no involvement in AAO or LCP offending and drug use. In addition, negative binomial regression results are relatively simple to interpret by exponentiating coefficients creating odds ratios that can be interpreted as each unit increase in the independent variable translates into a percent increase or decrease in offending.

A series of negative binomial regression models designed to examine the effects of delayed turning points and social bonds on offending will be run separately for both "AAO" and "LCP" outcomes. The focus on the study is how the delay of these turning points influences low-level "arrested adolescent" offenders. However, it is of value to study the role these factors have (or do not have) on more serious (LCP) offenders.

To test the twelve main hypotheses, multivariable analysis will be run at wave 3 using the Arrested Adolescent Offending scale/outcome variable. However, this study is also interested in related levels of low level drug use, as well the influence of the independent variables discussed have on life course persistent offending and drug use. In order to address these additional areas of interest, multivariate analysis will also be run using the Arrested Adolescent Drug Use, Life Course Persistent Offending, and Life Course Persistent Drug Use scales.

In order to examine the influence that emerging adulthood may have on abstainers who start offending as "late bloomers," an additional set of models will be run with all wave 3 outcome variables (AAO crime/AAO drug use, LCP crime/LCP drug use). A filter variable will be used to select those who scored "0" at wave 2, but scored a "1" or above on the offending scale to test hypothesis 12. An additional filter variable will be created to select those who are abstainers at wave 3 so that hypotheses 1 through 10 can also be tested for abstainers (see Appendix E).

MISSING VALUES ANALYSES

Prior studies using Add Health data have employed different strategies to compensate for missing data. Some scholars have imputed missing values (e.g., Haynie et al., 2008); other researchers have censured missing data by incorporating it for weighting purposes but removing it to compute parameter estimates (Haynie & Piquero, 2006). Prior studies using Add Health that performed analyses with both primary and imputed/weighted data found that there was little variation in the results (Haynie & McHugh, 2003). Consequently, multivariate analyses for this study will be conducted using imputed data.

The Missing Values module for SPSS v.17 was used to analyze and impute missing data values for independent variables. It was decided missing values for the outcomes would not be imputed in order to prevent changes in the distribution of the outcomes. Crime and drug use are relatively rare events compared to the independent variables, and imputing any values for the outcomes may have made them less representative of actual rates of offending and drug use in the Add Health sample. Further, it is generally advised not to impute data for outcomes (SPSS Missing Values Analysis, 2007). There are several steps involved in the process; the first step is the identification of the pattern of missing data as either missing completely at random (MCAR) or missing at random (MAR) (Allison, 2001). SPSS can identify patterns as MCAR or MAR using Little's chi-square statistic test. The null hypothesis for the Little's test is that the data are MAR, and results significant at the .05 level (SPSS Missing Values Analysis, 2007, p. 7). Data are MAR if the pattern of missing data is not completely random. Allison (2001) explains MAR by providing the following example of satisfying the MAR assumption "…missing data on income depended on a person's marital status, but within each marital status category, the probability of missing income was unrelated to income" (p.4). The data can be identified as are MCAR if, "the probability of missing data on Y is unrelated to the value of Y….or any other variables in the dataset" (Allison, 2001, p. 3). In other words, the information that is missing for that variable is independent of the value of other variables in the dataset. Once the pattern of missing data has been identified, the next step of the Missing Values procedure can be conducted which is deleting or imputing the data.

Data that are MCAR can be removed using simple procedures to perform both listwise and pairwise deletion. Listwise deletion involves deleting any observations that do not have complete data. There are two advantages to using this technique: first, it can be employed for any type of statistical analysis, and secondly it doesn't require any additional computations (cases are simply removed) (Allison, 2001). The main disadvantage is that listwise deletion decreases sample size (Pallant, 2007). Pairwise deletion excludes cases from any analysis involving variables for which they have missing data, however this technique is not considered advantageous because estimated errors and test statistics produced using the data are biased (Allison, 2001; Norusis, 2000).

If the data are not MCAR, Expectation-Maximization (EM) estimation must be used (SPSS Missing Values Analysis, 2007). The EM method consists of multiple iterations of data that have both an "E" step and an "M" step. During the "E" step iterations of data are processed, providing the conditional expectation of the 'missing data' based on the observed values and existing estimates of the parameters (SPSS Missing Values Analysis, 2007, p.7). The expectations from the "E" step are then used to replace the missing data. During the "M" step, maximum likelihood estimates of the parameters are tabulated as if the missing data has been replaced (SPSS Missing Values Analysis, 2007, p.7).

The Missing Values analysis revealed that data at each wave were not MCAR. For those variables with missing values (see Tables 7-9), values were imputed using the abovementioned Expectation-Maximization (EM) estimation procedure. Individual imputed data files for all 3 waves of data were saved and used for further analysis.

SUMMARY

This section has provided an overview of the Add Health data, the independent and dependent variables, discussed the hypotheses of this study, and have detailed the missing values analysis. Further, at all 3 waves of data there were no signs of multicollinearity. Tolerance levels were above .10. Variance inflation factors, VIFs, were acceptable with no values greater than 4 (Pallant, 2007).

CHAPTER 4

Findings

This section covers, in order of each wave of data, the imputed univariate statistics, results from bivariate analysis, and results of the multivariate models.

WAVE 1 RESULTS

As stated in the prior section, missing values for the independent variables were imputed using the Missing Values Module for SPSS v. 17. The imputed frequencies, limited to the appropriate ages (11-18) are presented in Table 12.

Table 12. *Descriptives of Independent Variables at Wave 1 (N = 4576) (Ages 11-18 Only)*

Variable	Min	Max	Mean	SD
Attendance at Religious Services	0	3	1.48	0.92
Grade in School	7	12	9.04	1.40
Hours Worked Scale	0	90	18.77	23.74
Low-Self Control Scale	0	12	3.31	2.43
Parental Attachment Scale	2	20	18.46	2.14
Peabody Picture Vocabulary Test	14	140	101.16	14.57
School Attachment Scale	3	15	11.23	2.57

	Frequency	Percentage		
Marital Status:				
Not Married	4428	99.2		
Married	35	0.8		

The next stage of the analysis involved performing correlational analyses which provided a description of the strength and direction of the linear relationship between variables. Spearman rank order correlation was used for the data due to the continuous variables used and the non-normal distribution of the data (Pallant, 2007). Correlational analyses were run with all four outcome variables at wave 1 to test for multicollinearity and to provide an examination of the relationships between the independent and dependent variables at waves 1 (see Appendix D). The results of the correlational analyses found no multicollinearity. There were several statistically significant relationships found between the independent and dependent variables at wave 1 that are discussed in further detail in Appendix D.

WAVE 2 RESULTS

As stated in the previous section missing values for the independent variables were imputed using the Missing Values Module for SPSS v.17. The imputed frequencies, limited to the ages 11- 18) in order to focus on those who were in adolescences at wave 2, are presented in Table 13.

Table 13.   *Descriptives of Independent Variables at Wave 2 (N = 4576) Ages 11-18 Only*

Variable	Min	Max	Mean	SD
Attendance at Religious Services	1	4	2.99	1.06
Grade in School	7	13	9.99	1.42
Hours Worked Scale	0	90	24.97	26.08
Low-Self Control Scale	0	12	3.10	2.23
Parental Attachment Scale	2	20	15.30	4.43
School Attachment Scale	3	15	11.25	2.56
	Frequency	**Percentage**		
Have Any Children				
No	4504	98.4		
Yes	72	1.6		
Marital Status				
Not Married	4551	99.5		
Married	24	.5		

Correlational analyses were run separately with all four outcome variables at wave 2 to test for multicollinearity and examine the strength and the direction of the relationships between the continuous independent variables and each of the dependent variables. As with wave 1, r.o multicollinearity was found, and there were several significant relationships found between the independent and dependent variables at wave 2 (see Appendix D).

WAVE 3 RESULTS

As stated in the previous section missing values for the independent variables were imputed using the Missing Values Module for SPSS v.17. The imputed frequencies, limited to those aged 18- 25, are presented in Table 14.

Table 14. *Descriptives of Independent Variables at Wave 3 (N = 4796) (Ages 18-25 Only)*

Variable	Min	Max	Mean	SD
Attendance at Religious Services	0	6	2.12	1.95
Current Job Satisfaction	1	5	3.92	.90
Economic Instability	0	5	.44	.84
Highest Grade in School	6	22	13.22	1.99
Hours Worked Scale	3	90	36.80	12.48
Parental Attachment Scale	1	10	7.00	2.24
Property Owned Scale	0	5	2.74	1.33

	Frequency	Percentage
Currently Service in the Military		
No	4749	98.3
Yes	76	1.6
Have Any Children		
No	3340	69.2
Yes	1487	30.8
Marital Status		
Not Married	4028	83.4
Married	801	16.6

The next stage of the analysis involved performing correlational analyses which provided a description of the strength and direction of the linear relationship between variables. Correlational analyses were run with all four outcome variables at wave 3 (see Appendix D).

The next step of the analysis was to see if there were differences in the independent and dependent variables by offender group. Recall that one of the goals of this study was to identify the arrested adolescent offender and to examine if this group would participate in different types of offenses than LCPs. To address this goal Mann-Whitney U tests were used to examine median score differences on the z scored dependent variables for AAOs and LCPs. Mann Whitney U tests identify whether the differences between the groups on the dependent variables are statistically significant or simply occur by chance. This is of value to this study because it may support the idea that AAOs and LCPs are different groups of offenders that score differently on less v. more serious offending and less v. more serious drug use.

The results of the Mann Whitney U tests found significant differences between AAOs and LCPs on all 4 outcomes, supporting the hypotheses that they are separate groups with distinct offending patterns. The results of the Mann Whitney U tests are presented in Table 15.

Table 15.   *Mann Whitney U Test – Wave 3 Comparison of AAOs and LCPs on Dependent Variables*

	Arrested Adolescent Offenders		**Life Course Persistent Offenders**		**Significant Difference Between Groups**
	N	Median	N	Median	
Arrested Adolescent Offending Scale	516	-.206	306	.322	.000
Life Course Persistent Offending Scale	518	.184	306	1.22	.000
Arrested Adolescent Drugs Used Scale	516	.746	305	.746	.010
Life Course Persistent Drugs Used Scale	513	-.385	303	.975	.000

Note. Median scores were transformed to z-scores.

The results of the Mann-Whitney U tests found significant differences on all 4 of the outcome scales at wave 3 between arrested adolescent and life course persistent offenders. A Mann Whitney U test revealed a significant difference in the AAO offense scale for AAOs (*Md* = -.206, *n* = 516) and LCPs (*Md* = .322, *n* = 306), *U* = 55723.00, *z* = -7.591, *p* <.05, r = -265, with LCPS having a higher median score on the AAO offense scale. This finding was expected, as Moffitt (1993) theorized, LCPs would commit similar types of offenses as ALs, but at higher rates. The Mann Whitney U test revealed a significant difference on the LCP offending scale for AAOs *(Md* = .184, *N* = 518) and LCPs (*Md* = 1.22, *N* = 306), *U* =8675.00, *z* = -21.55, *p* <.05, *r* = -.751. As expected, LCPS had a higher median score on the LCP offense scale compared to AAOs. There was a significant difference of the AAO drug use scale for AAOs (*Md* =.746, *N* = 516) and LCPs (*Md* = .746, *N* = 305, *U* = 71401.50, *z* = -2.58, *p* <.05, *r* = -.090. Although there was a significant difference on the AAO drugs use scale for AAOs and LCPs, there was not a difference on the median score of both groups. It is possible for both groups to have similar or the same median score because the Mann Whitney U test examines the rank sum score as opposed to the median value (Pallant, 2007). The Mann Whitney U test revealed a significant difference on the LCP drugs used scale for AAOs (*Md* = -.385, *N* = 513) and LCPs (*Md* = .975, *N* =303), *U* = 59725.50, *z* = -.39, p <.05, r = - .224. Unlike the AAO drug use scale, LCPs had a higher median score on the LCP drug use scale; this was as expected, as LCPs be more likely to use harsher drugs more often than AAOs. The final sets of analyses examine the multivariate models used to test the remaining hypotheses.

Multivariate Analysis

Count models, a subset of response regression models, were used because the outcome variables consist of a discrete count of occurrences of an event, in this case either the number of offenses that have occurred in the past 12 months (both low and more serious) and the number of drugs used (less serious and more serious). The purpose of count models is to explain how often an event occurs (Hilbe, 2008).

A series of negative binomial regression models were used because of the over dispersion in dependent variables, Arrested Adolescent offending, Life Course Persistent offending, and Life Course Persistent drug use (Hilbe, 2008; Long & Freese, 2006; StataCorp, 2006). Poisson models were used for the models using the AAO drug use outcome.

Three separate models were computed for all the outcomes. Model one included demographic variables, age, gender, two dummy variables White (0 = all others; 1 = White) and Black (0 = all others; 1 = Black) capturing the unique effect of race, and two dummy variables controlling for the unique effect of being identified as an Arrested Adolescent Offender (0 = all others; 1 = AAOs) and Life Course Persistent Offender (0 = all others; 1 = LCPs). Model 2 added the effects of turning points on crime taking into consideration demographic characteristics. Model 3 added social bonds and controlled for demographic characteristics, as well as including the effects of turning points in the model.

A separate series of models were also specified using reduced data files containing only "late bloomer" offenders who began offending at wave 3 (but had been abstainers in the prior wave) and those who were identified as ALs at wave 2 and were still offending at wave 3, in order to test hypotheses 11 and 12. The results of the first series of models, testing the core hypotheses of this study, are presented in Table 16.

Table 16.   *Negative Binomial Regression Models of Independent Variables on the Arrested Adolescent Offending Scale*

AAO Offending Scale	Model 1			Model 2			Model 3		
	B	(SE)	IRR	B	(SE)	IRR	B	(SE)	IRR
Age	-.085	.021	.918**	-.080	.023	.924**	-.099	.023	.905**
Gender	-.538	.075	.584**	-.553	.077	.574**	-.608	.078	.544**
Black	-.013	.133	.987	-.024	.114	.975	-.026	.114	.974
White	-.074	.097	.929	-.101	.098	.903	-.111	.098	.894
AAOs	1.29	.096	3.61**	1.29	.096	3.62**	1.23	.096	3.43**
LCPs	2.19	.106	8.96**	2.19	.106	9.01**	2.11	.106	8.22**
Military				.041	.288	1.04	.074	.283	1.08
Children				-.070	.091	.932	-.108	.091	.897
Education				.047	.205	1.05*	.069	.022	1.07**
Hours Worked				-.008	.004	.992*	-.008	.004	.911*

Table 17. *Negative Binomial Regression Models of Independent Variables on the Arrested Adolescent Offending Scale (Continued)*

AAO Offending Scale	Model 1			Model 2			Model 3		
Married				-.184	.124	.832	-.170	.127	.843
Religious Services							-.042	.020	.958*
Economic Instability							.310	.057	1.36**
Job Satisfaction							-.050	.040	.950
Parental Attachment							-.115	.037	.890**
Property Owned							.074	.073	1.08
Constant	.438	.468		.064	.501		.523	.538	
*p<.05	Chi–Square = 645.03			Chi–Square= 664.22			Chi–Square= 720.17		
**p<.01	Df = 6			Df=11			Df=16		
	Log likelihood = -3080.81			Log likelihood = -3071.22			Log likelihood = 3039.57		
	AIC = 1.288			AIC = 1.286			AIC = 1.277		

The economic instability, parental attachment, and property owned scales were z scored and mean summed. AIC stands for Aikake Information Criterion and is based on the log-likelihood function and is a measure of model fit. Models with the smallest value are considered to have the best fit (Hilbe, 2008)

Parameters are presented as incident rate ratios (IRR) given their relative ease of interpretation. For example, an IRR of 3.0 would suggest a one unit change in the independent variable would be expected to increase the average predicted count on the dependent variable by a factor of 3.0, while holding all independent variables constant. In contrast, an IRR of .50 would indicate that a one unit change in the independent variable would be expected to decrease the average predicted count on the dependent variable by a factor of .50, while holding all other independent variables constant (Long & Fresse, 2006).

<u>Demographics</u>

Model 1 included only the demographic variables being controlled for in the analysis and the variables representing membership in the AAO and LCP offending groups. In regards to age, for every one year increase in age there was an 8.2% decrease in the rate of AAO offenses (p<.05, IRR = .918), while holding all other variables in the model constant. Gender also was significant, with females having a 41.6% lower rate of AAO offenses compared to males (p<.01, IRR = .584). Both dummy variables for AAOs and LCPs were significant in model 1. AAOs had an expected crime court between three and four times larger than the expected count of non-AAOs (p<.01, IRR = 3.61). LCPs expected crime count was almost 9 times larger than that of other groups (p<.01, IRR = 8.96).

The results of model 1 were consistent with the hypothesized relationships between the demographic variables and AAO offending. As age increased, rates of AAO offending dropped as expected. Females, relative to males had lower rates of AAO offending, and both variables representing AAOs and LCPs were significant, with LCPs having higher counts of expected AAO offending. This finding was expected, as LCPs were hypothesized by Moffitt (1993) as participating in both less and more serious offenses at rates higher than ALs.

<u>Turning Points</u>

Model 2 added indicators of traditional turning points. The only turning points that were significant were education and hours worked per week. For participants having higher levels of education there was a 4% increase in the rate of AAO offenses for every year of additional education, (p<.05, IRR = 1.04). This result was surprising, as it was expected that having higher levels of education would inhibit offending, a hypotheses supporting by ample prior research (e.g., Lochner & Moretti, 2004). Hours worked per week were also significant. For every additional hour worked there was a decrease in the rate of AAO offending of .8%, holding all other variables constant (p<.05, IRR = .992).

The effect of age decreased slightly in model two. For every one year increase in age there was a 7.6% decrease in the rate of AAO offenses (p<.01, IRR = .924). There was a slight increase for gender, with females having a 42.6% lower rate of AAO offending compared to males (p<.01, IRR = .575). Both variables for AAOs and LCPs remained significant in model 2. AAOs had a expected rate of AAO offending between three and four times greater than others (p<.01, IRR

= 3.62). LCPs, had a rate of AAO offending approximately nine times higher than others (p<.01, IRR = 9.01).

In sum, the findings regarding turning points found only two hypothesized relationships significant. Education (hypothesis 5, page, 69) was in the opposite direction hypothesized. Hypothesis three (page. 69) that predicted working more hours would reduce rates of offending was supported.

Social Bonds

Model 3 added indicators of traditional social bonds. Several of the indicators of social bonds that were included in the model were significant, including economic instability, parental attachment, and religious participation. In addition, the relationships between age, gender, the AAO and LCP variables, education, and hours worked per week remained significant. Economic instability (reverse coded, higher score = lower levels of economic stability) had the strongest impact of the social bonds. For every one unit standard deviation increase in the economic instability scale, there was a 36% increase in the rate of AAO offenses (p<.01, IRR = 1.36). Parental bonds had the next strongest influence, with an 11% decrease in the incidence of AAO offending for every one unit increase in parental bonds (p<.01, IRR = .890). Religious participation was also significant. For every one unit increase in religious participation, there was a 4.2% decrease in the incidence of AAO offending (p<.05, IRR = .958). As in models 1 and 2, age and gender were both significant in the final model. For every additional year in age, there was a 9.5% decrease in the incidence of AAO offending (p<.01, IRR = .905). Females, compared to males, had a 45.6% lower rate of AAO offending (p<.01, IRR = .545). Both dummy variables for AAOs and LCPs remained significant in model 3. AAOs compared to others, while holding all other variables constant in the model, are expected to have a rate of AAO offending between three and four times greater than others (p<.01, IRR = 3.43). LCPs had a rate of AAO offending between eight and nine times higher than other groups (p<.01, IRR = 8.22). The distinction between AAOs and LCPs was important because it demonstrated that AAOs and LCPs have different rates of offending. Further, LCPs were expected to commit higher rates of offenses overall, both less and more serious offenses, so the higher rates of LCP offending reported here were expected.

Education remained significant when social bonds were added. For every additional year of education, there was a 7% increase in the rate of AAO offending (p<.01, IRR = 1.07). Hours worked per week was also significant while holding all other variables in the model constant, There was a .8% decrease in the rate of AAO offending for every hour worked (p<.05, IRR = .992). In sum, several of the hypothesized relationships dealing with social bonds and AAO offending were supported. Consistent with hypothesis seven (page 69), religious participation predicted lower levels of AAO offending. Hypothesis eight that predicted an increase in parental bonds to parents would also be related to lower levels of AAO offending was supported. Finally, hypothesis nine that predicted higher levels of economic instability would be related to increased AAO offending was also supported. The next series of models examined the demographic variables, turning points, and social bond indicators using the LCP offending outcome (reported in Table 17).

Table 18.   *Negative Binomial Regression Models of Independent Variables on the Life Course Persistent Offending Scale*

LCP Offending Scale	Model 1			Model 2			Model 3		
	B	(SE)	IRR	B	(SE)	IRR	B	(SE)	IRR
Age	-.026	.013	.974	-.020	.014	.980	-.021	.014	.979
Gender	-.138	.053	.871**	-.129	.055	.879*	-.141	.056	.868*
Black	.084	.067	1.09	.078	.068	1.08	.070	.069	1.07
White	-.036	.060	.964	-.027	.061	.974	-.010	.062	.989
AAOs	20.8	477.2	1.08	20.8	499.1	1.17	21.1	562.7	1.47
LCPs	22.01	477.2	3.65	22.1	499.1	3.94	22.3	562.7	4.96
Military				.099	.139	1.10	.116	.140	1.12
Children				.018	.059	1.02	.026	.059	1.03
Education				-.018	.012	.981	-.012	.014	.988
Hours Worked				.001	.002	1.01	.001	.002	1.01
Married							-.061	.101	.940
Religious Services							.003	.014	1.01

Table 19. *Negative Binomial Regression Models of Independent Variables on the Life Course Persistent Offending Scale (Continued)*

LCP Offending Scale	Model 1		Model 2		Model 3		
Economic Instability					-.007	.034	.992
Job Satisfaction					-.029	.025	.971
Parental Attachmen					-.015	.024	.985
Property Owned					-.067	.045	.935
Constant	-19.9	477.2	-19.8	499.1	-20.2	562.7	
*p<.05	Chi – Square = 4629.8		Chi – Square = 4633.9		Chi – Square = 4623.5		
**p<.01	Df = 5		Df = 10		Df = 15		
	Log likelihood = -1223.45		Log likelihood = -1221.36		Log likelihood = -1213.79		
	AIC = .513		AIC = .514		AIC = .514		

The economic instability, parental attachment, and property owned scales were z scored and mean summed.

Life Course Persistent Outcome

Demographics

Model 1 included only the demographic variables being controlled for in the analysis and the variables representing membership in the AAO and LCP offending groups. Gender was the only significant predictor, with females compared to males having a 12.7% (p<.05, IRR = .871) lower rate of LCP offending.

Turning Points

Indicators of traditional turning points were entered into the next model. Of the indicators added, none had a significant relationship with counts of life course persistent offenses. The impact of gender remained significant, with females compared to males having a 12.1% lower rate of LCP offending (p<.05, IRR = .879).

Social Bonds

The final model run with the life course persistent offending outcome added indicators of traditional social bonds. None of the indicators of social bonds that were included in the model were significant. However, the impact of gender remained, with females having a 13.02% lower rate of LCP offending compared to males (p<.01, IRR, .868). The next series of models examined the demographic variables, turning points, and social bonds using the AAO drug use outcome (see Table 18).

Table 20. *Poisson Regression Models of Independent Variables on the Arrested Adolescent Offending Drug Use Scale*

AAO Drugs Used Scale	Model 1			Model 2			Model 3		
	B	(SE)	IRR	B	(SE)	IRR	B	(SE)	IRR
Age	.005	.006	1.01	.007	.006	1.01	-.001	.006	.999
Gender	-.038	.021	.962	-.034	.022	.966	-.025	.022	.974
Black	-.196	.034	.822**	-.204	.034	.815**	-.173	.035	.840**
White	.085	.028	1.09**	.081	.028	1.08**	.066	.028	1.06*
AAOs	.262	.031	1.30**	.258	.031	1.29**	.232	.032	1.26**
LCPs	.321	.038	1.38**	.317	.039	1.37**	.281	.039	1.32**
Military				-.105	.087	.900	-.111	.087	.894
Children				-.009	.026	.990	-.021	.026	.979
Education				.006	.005	1.01	.015	.006	1.01*
Hours Worked				.001	.001	1.00	.001	.001	1.00
Married				-.089	.031	.914**	-.066	.033	.936*
Religious Services							-.048	.006	.953**
Economic Instability							.046	.017	1.05**

Table 21. *Poisson Regression Models of Independent Variables on the Arrested Adolescent Offending Drug Use Scale (Continued)*

AAO Drugs Used Scale	Model 1		Model 2		Model 3		
Job Satisfaction					-.018	.011	.982
Parental Attachment					-.029	.010	.971
Property Owned					.050	.021	1.05**
Constant	.512	.133	.389	.142	.616	.154	
*p<.05	Chi – Square = 243.6		Chi – Square = 258.9		Chi – Square = 360.2		
**p<.01	Df = 6		Df = 11		Df = 16		
	Log likelihood = - 7293.60		Log likelihood = - 7285.96		Log likelihood = - 7222.27		
	AIC = 3.04		AIC = 3.04		AIC = 3.02		

The economic instability, parental attachment, and property owned scales were z scored and mean summed.

Arrested Adolescent Drug Use Outcome

A Poisson regression model was used for the models using the AAO drug use outcome variable, due to few zero scores in the distribution. Three separate models were completed. Model one included demographic variables, age, gender, two dummy variables capturing the unique effect of race, and two dummy variables representing being either an AAO or an LCP. Model 2 looked at the effects of turning points on crime, taking into consideration demographic characteristics. Model 3 added social bonds and controlled for demographic characteristics, as well as including the effects of turning points in the model.

Demographics

Model 1 included only the demographic variables being controlled for in the analysis and the variables representing membership in the AAO and LCP offending groups. Both race variables and both offending variables were significant. Blacks, as compared to other groups, had a 17.8% lower rate of AAO drug use (p<.01, IRR = .822). In contrast, whites, compared to other groups, had a 9% higher rate of AAO drug use (p<.01, IRR = 1.09). Both dummy variables for AAOs and LCPs were significant in model 1. AAOs, compared to others had between one and two times larger expected count of AAO drug use (p<.01, IRR = 1.30). LCPs had between one and two times the expected count of AAO drug use, compared to others (p<.01, IRR = 1.40).

The findings dealing with demographics found that Blacks had lower rates of AAO drug use, and conversely, whites had higher rates. Both AAOs and LCPs had similar expected counts of AAO drug use.

Turning Points

Indicators of traditional turning points were entered into the next model. Of the indicators added, only marital status had a significant effect, with those who were married, compared to those who were single, having a 8.6% decrease in AAO drug use (p<.01, IRR = .914). Both race variables and the offender category variables remained significant with the addition of turning points. Blacks, as compared to other groups, had an 18.5% lower rate of AAO drug use (p<.01, IRR = .815). Conversely, whites, as compared to other groups, had an 8% increase in the rate of AAO drug use (p<.01, IRR = 1.08). AAOs, as compared to other groups, had between one and two times the expected count of AAO drug use (p<.01, IRR = 1.29) compared to other groups. LCPs had an expect count of AAO drug use between eight and nine times higher than other groups (p<.01, IRR = .815).

Consistent with hypothesis one (page 69) marital status was found to be related to AAO drug use, with those who are married having lower rates of AAO drug use. None of the other turning points controlled for in the model were statistically significant.

Social Bonds

Indicators of social bonds were added to model 3. Several of the indicators of social bonds that were included in model were significant including religious participation, economic instability, parental attachment, and property owned. In addition, both race variables, as well as both offending categories, remained significant. Marital status remained significant, and education was also significant in this model.

Economic instability and property owned were the variables with the strongest relationships. For economic instability, there was a 5% increase in AAO drug use for every one unit increase in economic instability (reverse coded) (p<.01, IRR = 1.05). In regards to property owned, there was a 5% increase in AAO drug use for every increase in the amount of property owned (p<.05, IRR = 1.05). Religious participation was the next strongest indicator. There was a 4.2% decrease in the rate of AAO drug use (p<.01, IRR = .942) for every 1 unit increase in religious participation. The final social bond that was significant was parental attachment. There was a 2.9% decrease in the incidence of AAO drug use for every one unit increase in parental attachment (p<.01, IRR = .971). Of the demographic variables, both race variables and both offending category variables remained significant, though the strength of the relationships were slightly weaker with the introduction of the social bond indicators. Blacks, as compared to other groups, had a 16% lower rate of AAO drug use (p<.01, IRR = .840). Conversely, whites, as compared to other groups, had a 6% increase in the rate of AAO drug use (p<.01, IRR = 1.06). AAOs had an expected count between one and two times higher than other groups (p<.01, IRR = 1.26). LCPs also had an expected count between one and two times higher than that of other groups on AAO drug use (p<.01, IRR = 1.32).

Two indicators of turning points, marital status and education, were significant in model 3. As in model 2, those who were married, as compared to those who were not, had a 6.5% decrease in the incident of AAO drug use (p<.05, IRR = .936). Unlike model 2, where education was not significant, education was significant with the additional of social bond variables, with there being a 1% increase in the incident of AAO drug use for every year of additional education (p <.05, IRR = 1.01).

In sum, of the hypotheses examining social bonds included in the models examining AAO drug use, several were supported. Consistent with hypothesis seven, religious participation was found to reduce AAO drug use. Hypothesis eight was supported, with increases in parental attachment decreasing AAO drug use. Consistent with hypothesis eight, higher levels of economic instability were found to predict increases in AAO drug use. Finally, hypothesis ten, that predicted owning more property would decrease offending (in this case AAO drug use) was significant, but in the opposite direction hypothesized. The next series of models examined the demographic variables, turning points, and social bond indicators and how they predicted LCP drug use (see Table 19).

Table 22.   *Negative Binomial Regression Models of Independent Variables on the Life Course Persistent Drugs Use Scale*

LCP Drugs Used Scale	Model 1			Model 2			Model 3		
	B	(SE)	IRR	B	(SE)	IRR	B	(SE)	IRR
Age	.226	.018	1.03	.055	.019	1.06**	.036	.019	1.04
Gender	-.103	.067	.901	-.074	.068	.928	-.059	.068	.941
Black	-1.23	.138	.293**	-1.25	.137	.285**	-.122	.138	.293**
White	.331	.084	1.39**	.332	.084	1.39**	.311	.084	1.39**
AAOs	.944	.087	2.57**	.896	.086	2.45**	.818	.086	2.26**
LCPs	1.54	.092	4.68**	1.49	.091	4.45**	1.40	.090	4.04**
Military				-.378	.289	.685	-.358	.286	.699
Children				-.073	.082	.930	-.116	.082	.890
Education				-.028	.017	.972	.007	.018	1.01
Hours Worked				-.002	.003	.998	-.001	.003	.998
Married				-.515	.109	.598**	-.366	.113	.693**
Religious Services							-.118	.019	.888**
Economic Instability							.102	.049	1.10*
Job Satisfaction							-.078	.034	.924*
Parental Attachment							-.112	.032	.893**
Property Owned							-.060	.063	.941
Constant	-2.41	.418		-2.36	.442		-1.93	.470	
*p<.05	Chi – Square = 506.9			Chi – Square = 539.2			Chi – Square = 612.3		
**p<.01	Df = 6			Df = 11			Df = 16		
	Log likelihood = - 2796.26			Log likelihood = - 2780.10			Log likelihood = - 2736.80		
	AIC = 1.18			AIC = 1.17			AIC = 1.15		

The economic instability, parental attachment, and property owned scales were z scored and mean summed.

Life Course Persistent Drug Use Outcome

<u>Demographics</u>

Model 1 included only the demographic variables being controlled for in the analysis and the variables representing membership in the AAO and LCP offending groups. Both race variables and both offending variables were significant. Blacks, as compared to other groups, had a 70.7% lower rate of LCP drug use (p<.01, IRR = .293). In contrast, whites, compared to other groups, had a 39% higher incident rate of LCP drug use (p<.01, IRR = 4.68). Both dummy variables for AAOs and LCPs were significant in model 1. AAOs compared to others (LCPs and abstainers) had between two and three times higher rate of LCP drug use (p<.01, IRR = 2.57). LCPs had an expected count between four and five times higher than other groups on LCP drug use (p<.01, IRR = 4.68).

As with the models dealing with the AAO drug out outcome, both variables dealing with race and offender type were significant. Similar to the results with AAO drug outcome, Blacks had lower rates of LCP drug use, and whites had higher rates. LCPs, as expected, had the highest expect count of LCP drug use.

<u>Turning Points</u>

Indicators of traditional turning points were entered into the next model. Of the indicators added, only marital status had a significant relationship. Those who were married, as compared to those who were single had a 40.20% lower rate of LCP drug use (p<.01, IRR = .598).

The relationship with race was also significant in this model, with Blacks having a 71.5% lower incidence of LCP drug use compared with other racial groups(p<.01, IRR = .286). Whites, as compared to other groups, had the opposite relationship, showing a 39% increase in the incidence of LCP drug use (p<.01, IRR = 1.39). In this model age was significant; for every one year increase in age there was a 6% decrease in the rate of LCP drug use (p<.05, IRR = 1.06). Both offender categories were significant predictors. AAOs had almost two and half times the expected count of LCP drug use compared to other groups (p<.01, IRR = 2.45). LCPs had an expected count of LCP drug use almost four and half times higher than other groups (p<.01, IRR = 4.45).

<u>Social Bonds</u>

Indicators of social bonds were added to model 3. Several of the indicators of social bonds that were included in model were significant including religious participation, economic stability, parental attachment, job satisfaction. In addition, both race variables as well as both offending categories remained significant. Marital status remained significant as well. Religious participation had the strongest relationship, with an 11.2% decrease in the incidence of LCP drug use for every one unit increase in religious participation (p<.01, IRR = .888). Parental attachment had the next strongest effect. For every one unit increase, there was a 10.6% decrease in LCP drug use (p<.01, IRR = .893). Economic instability (reverse scored) was the next strongest predictor; For every one unit increase in the level of economic (in)stability, there was a 10% increase in the amount of LCP drug use(p<.05, IRR = 1.11). Job satisfaction was the final social bond indicator that was significant. There was a 7.6% reduction in LCP drug use for every one unit increase in job satisfaction (p<.05, IRR = .924).

Race remained significant in this model, with Blacks having a 70.7% lower incidence LCP drug use compared with other racial groups (p<.01, IRR = .293). Whites, compared to other groups, had the opposite relationship, having a 39% increase in the incidence of LCP drug use (p<.01, IRR = 1.39). In this model age was no longer significant. Both offender categories variables remained significant with AAOs, had between two and three times higher the expected count of LCP drug use compared to other groups (p<.01, IRR = 2.26). LCPs had over four times the expected count of LCP drug use (p<.01, IRR = 4.04) compared to other groups.

Marital status was the only social bond that remained significant in the third model. Those who were married, compared with those who were not, had a 30.7% decrease in the rate of LCP drug use (p<.01, IRR = .694).

In sum, several of the social bonds examined in this model were found to have significant relationships with LCP drug use. Consistent with hypothesis six, higher levels of job satisfaction lead to a reduction in LCP drug use. Hypothesis seven was supported, with higher levels of religious participation leading to lower levels of LCP drug use.

Higher levels of parental attachment (hypothesis eight) were found to reduce LCP drug use. Finally, hypothesis nine was also supported, with higher levels of economic instability found to be related to increased LCP drug use.

To examine hypotheses 11 and 12 a series of models were run to examine the role of demographic factors, turning points, and indicators of social bonds. The detailed results of these analyses are located in Appendix E.

CHAPTER 5

Discussion

Using bivariate and multivariate analysis of three waves of Add Health data, the previous section explored the relationships between demographic characteristics, traditional indicators of turning points, and social bonds, low level offending and more serious offending, and low level and more serious drug use. By using bivariate analysis on the earlier waves of data these analyses expanded the scope of the theory of emerging adulthood by investigating possible changes in traditional turning points and social bonds earlier in the life course. The analyses conducted at wave 3 expanded the theory of emerging adulthood by applying it directly to criminal offending and drug use while controlling for offender typology. The result of these analyses suggest that key indicators of turning points (e.g., education, marital status, and hours worked per week) and social bonds (e.g., religious participation, economic stability, parental attachment, property owned, and job satisfaction) had relationships with low and high level offending, and low and high level drug use that were both consistent with several key hypotheses and inconsistent with others. The discussion will begin by examining how the separating of the AAOs and LCPs was of value to this study. The results related to the demographic variables will then be discussed, following by the hypotheses related to turning points, and the hypotheses related to social bonds. The implications of identifying AAOs for theory, the criminal justice system, and policy will then be discussed.

AAOS VS. LCPS

This study was the first to identify a new offender typology, the arrested adolescent offender, by building on the conceptual foundation of offender taxonomies developed by Moffitt (1993). As discussed in chapter 3, AAOs were identified using a methodology employed by other scholars (Barnes & Beaver, 2010) to identify ALs. Approximately 11% of the sample was identified as AAOs and 6% were identified as LCPs. Identifying and separating AAOs and LCPs was useful for this study because it allowed a comparison of the rate of offending for each group, with results indicating that AAOs commit fewer offenses and have a lower incidence rate of both low (AAO) and more serious drug use (LCP).

It was theorized that the arrested adolescent offender would commit fewer and less serious crimes than LCPs. This hypothesized relationship was supported in the first series of models dealing with the AAO outcome (Table 16) where LCPs had higher rates of AAO offending, as well as AAO drug use (Table 18), and LCP drug use (Table 19). Moffitt (1993) argued that LCPs would commit many of the same offenses as ALs, as well as more serious offenses. The findings of this study support Moffitt's (1993) offender typology and provide a framework that can be utilized in future studies examining AAOs and LCPs.

Curiously, the distinction between AAOs and LCPs was not useful in predicting LCP offending. As expected, being an AAO was not a predictor of LCP offending. However, being identified as an LCP was not a predictor of LCP offending; this was the opposite of what was expected. Recall that LCPs were identified as those who scored in the upper 5th percent of the serious offending scale (N = 306) and AAOs the lower 95th percentile (N = 518). There were significantly less LCPs relative to AAOs in the sample, thus the majority of the offenses committed were most likely committed by AAOs. The importance of the identification of AAOs will be discussed relative to specific hypotheses and policy and theory issues over the next sections.

DEMOGRAPHICS

Age, gender, and race were included in the analysis as statistical controls. The relationship between age and offending varied across analytic technique and wave of the data. At all three waves, some of the dependent variables had a relationship with age, all of which were in the expected direction. For example, at wave 1 age had a significant positive relationship with all four outcomes. Members of the sample who were older scored higher on all the outcome scales. This was expected, as older participants would be closer to the peak years of offending (14-17 years old) (Gottfredson & Hirschi, 1990).

At wave 2, age correlated only with the AL and LCP drug outcome variables. This finding was surprising as it would be expected that the relationship between age and offending would remain as the sample ages and moves closer to the peak years of offending. A possible explanation is that during this stage drug experimentation is common among young people. For example, the 2007 arrest rates for drug law violations for youth was nearly double that of 1990 (Puzzanchera, 2009). This demonstrates that drug offending is becoming increasingly more common amongst younger people.

An alternative explanation may have to do with public backlash against juvenile crime and the use of such initiatives as curfews to curtail juvenile delinquency and crime. As a result, greater attention may have been paid to adolescents during their most crime prone years by both informal and formal agents of social control. This would coincide with the general shift from a due process to more crime control oriented model. This is of course, only speculation, but it does present a possible explanation as to why there were not significant relationships between age and the crime outcomes at wave 2.

The most important findings for this study regarding the relationship between age and offending were found at wave 3. There was a significant negative relationship found between AAO and LCP offending. This supports the hypothesized relationship whereby offending would decrease as people age. More importantly, age was a significant predictor of AAO offending in all 3 regression models (see Table 16), indicating that age is a relevant factor for predicting low-level offending and that it can be expected that rates of low-level offending will decrease as people age. This supports prior research that argues low-level offending decreases as people age, and that more serious offending continues for a longer period of time over the life course. Further, these results lend support to Gottfredson and Hirschi's (1990) discussion that the age crime curve is invariant, and that changing social circumstances such as emerging adulthood would not alter the relationship between age and offending.

As discussed in chapter 1, the relationship between age and crime is one of the most consistently found, yet hotly debated issues. Although it was certainly not the focus of this study to test the age-crime curve, it was of interest to study if there would be a relationship between age and offending for those experiencing the new stage of emerging adulthood. The role of age is an important factor with offending over the life course and as future waves of these data are collected and analyzed, it will be of interest to see how emerging adulthood influences offending. The current data prevent a longitudinal analysis examining age, as there is only one wave of data collected from the sample during the critical stage of emerging adulthood thereby limiting generalizations to subsequent waves when participants are older.

As with age, gender was included in these analyses as a control variable. Gender was of interest because prior research (e.g., Laub & Sampson, 2003) was limited to male samples. It was also of interest to examine if prior findings regarding female criminality such as Moffitt's et al. (2001) who found female offending peaks in early puberty would be applicable for those who have experienced emerging adulthood.

Gender was a significant predictor for the models using both the AAO offending and LCP offending outcomes, with being female predicting lower levels of offending across all models. These findings support the hypothesized relationship that being female would reduce rates of offending. These findings also provide an indicator that traditional turning points and social bonds still "work" for females. Further, despite increases in the overall rate of female offending in recent years (Belknap, 2007), the findings of this study support prior research that female criminality peaks early in the life course and women still offend less than men.

Unlike gender, race was not a significant predictor of AAO or LCP offending at wave 3. This may indicate that race has no influence on offending for those in emerging adulthood. However, race was a significant predictor of both AAO and LCP drug use, with Blacks having lower counts of both low and more serious drug use. Initially, this finding was surprising, as Blacks have higher rates of arrest and incarceration for drug crimes. However, this finding supports data reported in the *National Household Survey on Drug Use and Health, 2005,* and other studies that have found Blacks have lower rates of drug use than Whites and other racial/ethnic groups (e.g., Mumola & Karberg, 2006).

The remainder of this chapter is devoted to discussing the results of the hypotheses presented in chapter 3, and the implications that can be drawn from these findings. Because both bivariate and multivariate analyses were conducted, the discussion will focus on key concepts directly related to the hypotheses tested.

TURNING POINTS

As discussed in chapter 2, turning points such as getting married, having children, and serving in military, gaining higher levels of education, and working more hours have traditionally acted as informal social controls, inhibiting crime and deviance (e.g., Laub and Sampson).

The relationship between marriage and Arrested Adolescent offending (hypothesis 1) was not supported. Marriage was also not a significant predictor of LCP offending. However, marriage was a significant predictor of both AAO and LCP drug use.

Taken as a whole, these findings suggest that marital status is no longer a relevant predictor of either low or more serious offending. This was not surprising. As discussed in chapter 2, many in the stage of emerging adulthood postpone marriage until later in the life course. This may prevent marriage from acting as turning point, at least between the ages of 18 and 25. It is possible that marriage may be a significant predictor of AAO offending as the sample ages. Marriage was a significant predictor for both drug outcomes; this suggests that while not relevant for offending, marriage does act as a turning point for some behaviors, decreasing drug use. While this finding does not support the hypothesis that marriage reduces offending for AAOs, it does suggest that marriage still has some ability to inhibit some forms of deviant behavior, in this case drug use. It should also be noted that the models examining the relationship between marriage, offending and drug use, using the sub-sample of "persisters," or "late bloomers" (hypotheses 11 and 12, page 68) were not supported.

An alternative explanation may be that marriage may not be the only form of romantic relationship that may have a role in inhibiting crime or drug use. This study focused on marriage because it was the most socially accepted relationship for the men in the Laub and Sampson's sample. However, for those born since 1960 there has been a marked increase in cohabitation. Further, same–sex relationships were not examined. These relationships may act as turning points for emerging adults and may be important factors to consider as research in this area continues. Further, scholars in both the sociological and public health literatures have found that marriage acts differently for males and females, benefitting males with both more stable physical and mental health but often affecting females negatively (e.g., increases in stress levels). It is possible that marriage may act as a positive turning point for males, but may not have the same (or any) influence on female criminality. Future studies may want to examine the possible interaction between gender and marital status and how it may influence offending.

The relationship between having children and AAO offending (hypothesis 2; page 67) was not supported. This finding was surprising as it was expected that having children would act as a turning point and inhibit low-level offending. None of the other models using the LCP offending outcome, drug outcomes, or "late bloomer" or "persisting" offender subsamples found a significant relationship with having children. These findings suggest that being a parent is no longer as relevant a factor as is was for the men in Laub and Sampson's study for whom being a parent largely reduced offending. It is possible that like marriage, the delay in parenting that has occurred over the last few decades has altered the effectiveness of having children as a turning point. The utility of parenting as a turning point may not exhibit itself until later in the life course when more individuals in this sample have become parents.

Parenting may also act differently for a males and females. Traditionally, primary care giving has been the responsibility of females and thus may be more apt to turn female offenders away from crime and deviance. Studies in the life course literature (e.g., Laub & Sampson, 2003) have largely focused on male offenders. Future studies may want to examine the role of parenthood and gender as an interaction in order to study how parenthood operates as a turning point away from offending for males and females. Further, many who are parents during emerging adulthood may be living with their own parents and receiving assistance in providing care for their child. Prior research has found that there has been an increase in the number of grandmothers that provide supportive care for their grandchildren (Bayder & Brooks-Gunn, 1998), and that between 5-6% of children have grandparents living with them in their home (Perley & Rudkin, 1999). Having one's own parents assist with care giving may allow many emerging adult parents to have an additional level of personal freedom. This "freedom" could be used to participate in deviant or criminal behavior. Alternatively, having greater levels of freedom could be used for working more hours which could decrease bonds to family. Working more hours could also lead to increased levels of frustration and drug use. As with marriage, the influence of having children as a turning point may not be seen until later in the life course.

The relationship between working more hours and AAO offending (hypothesis 3; page 67) was supported with those working more hours having lower levels of AAO offending. Working more hours was not related to LCP offending, or AAO and LCP drug use. It is possible that working more hours was not related to LCP offending because LCPs may be less likely to work legitimate jobs. The relationship at earlier waves between hours worked and offending and drug use varied. At earlier waves of the data, correlational analyses with all 4 outcomes found that working more hours had a positive relationship with offending and drug use (wave 1). At wave 2 there was also a significant, positive correlation between hours worked with LCP offending, and AL and LCP drug use. These findings were surprising, as it would be expected that working more hours would prevent offending and drug use because working occupies time and workplace norms may act as a form of social control. Further, prior studies have found that those who have found that employment is negatively related to drug use (Gills & Michaels, 1992) and that drug use is typically higher in those who are unemployed (Normand, Lempert & O'Brien, 1994). However, it is possible that working more hours may simply translate to a higher income which may allow some to buy more drugs. Although this study did not include employment status as a variable, it could be argued that hours worked per week may act as a proxy for employment, and as such it would be expected that working more hours would reduce drug use. It should be noted that there were no statistically significant relationships found between hours worked and the outcome variables using the subsamples of "late bloomers" or "persisters."

The relationship between military service and offending (hypothesis 4) was not supported. None of the models run with the "late bloomers" or "persisters" subsamples revealed a significant relationship between military service and any of the outcome variables. This finding was not unexpected as only a small number of the participants (n = 76) were actively serving in the military at the time of the wave 3 data collection. It should be noted that the survey was collected in late 2001/early 2002. Waves 4 and 5 of the data will most likely contain significantly more individuals actively serving in the military due to the current Middle East crisis.

The diminished role of military service is interesting because prior studies found that military service acted as a turning point for most away from crime and deviance for the World War II generation, but was less effective for later generations (see chapter 2). What has yet to be explored thoroughly is how military service has affected emerging adults, particularly those serving in the Middle East. This current conflict, like Vietnam, has been contentious in general society, with many initially supporting military presence but as time has passed the presence of the military has become more controversial. Based on the findings of studies using samples of Vietnam veterans, it is possible that military service may act as a negative turning point for emerging adults. In contrast, public sentiment supporting the conflict in the Middle East has cooled over time, but overall support for those in the military has remained fairly consistent and they have yet to face the same level of vitriol from the public (e.g., protests against soldiers, refusal to hire veterans) that those who served in Vietnam experienced. As a result, modern veterans may not experience military service as a negative turning point. Empirical examination of such hypotheses should be possible when Waves 4 and 5 Add Health data are made available for researchers.

The final turning point theorized to influence AAO offending was education (hypothesis 5). The relationship between level of education and offending and education and drug use had a varied relationship that depended upon the analytic technique and the wave of data. The relationship between education and offending at wave 1 was consistently significant, but in an unexpected direction, with higher levels of education having a positive association with both AL and LCP offending, and AL and LCP drugs used. At wave 2 of the data education had a significant positive association with both AL and LCP drugs used, as with wave 1, this was also in an unexpected direction. None of the models ran with the subsamples of "late bloomers" or "persisters" revealed a significant relationship between education and any of the outcome variables.

These relationships may be explained by the aforementioned relationship between age and offending. As the sample aged they moved closer to the peak period of active offending (for lower level offenses), while concurrently moving up from grade to grade. Further, during the earlier waves participants were biologically maturing which, as Moffitt et al. (2001) argued, may influence offending.

At wave 3, the relationship between education and the AAO offending and drug use outcome were significant, with higher levels of education predicting higher levels of AAO offending and drug use. These relationships were surprising and in the opposite direction theorized. A possible explanation for these outcomes is that many of the participants may currently be enrolled in college, as discussed in chapters 1 and 2; low level offending and drug use are common among college aged individuals. Behaviors such as public drunkenness, being loud and rowdy, and the use of low-level drugs have all been thoroughly documented by prior studies.

Conversely, education was a predictor in models using the LCP offending outcome, with those who had higher levels of education having lower levels of LCP offenses. This supported the hypothesis that education would reduce LCP offending. This suggests that education does act as a turning point for more serious offenders. Further, this supports the logic for distinguishing between AAOs and LCPs.

Taken together these findings suggest that a relationship between education and offending and drug use exists, but is sensitive to the outcome variable being tested. The relationship between education and the outcomes had the clearest relationship at wave 1, with being in a higher grade being positively correlated with all 4 outcomes. This relationship became more muddled, switching directions depending on the outcome at wave 3. The next section examines the results of the hypotheses dealing with social bonds.

SOCIAL BONDS

As discussed in chapter 2, social bonds such as job satisfaction and religious participation have traditionally acted as informal social controls, inhibiting crime and deviance. The men in Laub and Sampson's sample identified social bonds as an important factor in their desistance. The hypothesized relationship between job satisfaction and arrested adolescent offending (hypothesis 6) was not supported. There was a significant relationship found between job satisfaction and LCP drug use, with greater levels of job satisfaction decreasing LCP drug use. Further, correlations between job satisfaction and the LCP offending, and both AAO and LCP drug use variables were significant, revealing that those who scored lower on job satisfaction had higher levels of LCP offending, and those who scored lower on job satisfaction scored higher on the drug use outcome scale. A significant relationship was also found between job satisfaction and LCP drug use, with a higher score on job satisfaction reducing the amount of LCP drug use. There were no significant findings between job satisfaction and any of the outcomes using the "late bloomer" or "persister" subsamples.

The totality of these findings reveal that while not supporting the core hypothesis that higher levels of job satisfaction would reduce AAO crime, the findings did find a significant negative relationship between job satisfaction and the remaining outcomes. Further, job satisfaction was found to be a significant predictor of LCP drug use. These findings suggest that job satisfaction may still be a valid social bond that may be used to inhibit offending and drug use. This relationship was clearest with the LCP drug use outcome. As with marital status and having children, it is possible that the role of job satisfaction may not be prevalent until later in the life course. Many in emerging adulthood are still in college and working lower level jobs where they may be experiencing less satisfaction than they would if they were in their chosen field. In other words, the effect of job satisfaction may be found when the sample is older and have attained employment in the career of their choice instead of the jobs that many have while in college. Alternatively, it may be possible that there may be a discrepancy between the employment expectations of emerging adults versus their actually ability to achieve employment that would provide them with higher levels of job satisfaction at this stage of the life course. The next social bond examined was religious participation.

The relationship between religious participation and offending and drug use (hypothesis 7, page 67) depended upon the wave of the data and the analytic technique. At wave 1, religious participation had a theoretically unexpected relationship, with higher levels of religious participation correlating with higher levels of AL offending and AL drug use. This may be explained by the age of the sample at this stage. Prior researchers (e.g., Kohlberg, 1959; Steinberg, 2005) have found that moral reasoning is a process that evolves as the brain develops. Youths at this stage may simply not have achieved the physiological development necessary for religious participation to be an effective social control.

At wave 2, the relationship between religious participation and the outcomes were in the expected direction. There were significant, negative correlations between religious participation and AL and LCP offending scales, and AL and LCP drug use scales. These relationships were expected, as prior studies have found that religious participation may inhibit criminality and deviance.

At wave 3, all four outcome variables were negatively correlated with religious participation. More importantly, hypothesis 6 was supported, with higher levels of religious participation predicting a reduction in AAO crime. Greater levels of religious participation also predicted a reduction in AAO drug use and LCP drug use. Religious participation was also found to be a significant predictor in the model using the "late bloomers" and the LCP drug use outcome, with higher levels of religious participation reducing LCP drug use.

The totality of these findings suggests that religious participation is most effective for older youths and young adults who commit low-level offenses. Religious participation was also effective at predicting a reduction in low and high level drug use. These findings support prior studies which found religious participation is an effective social bond capable of reducing low level crime and drug use for emerging adults. The next social bond examined was parental attachment.

Parental attachment was explored across all 3 waves of the data and had one of the clearest relationships with the outcome variables. Parental attachment was a significant predictor of reduced AAO offending (hypothesis 8). This finding was in the expected relationship and direction. Parental attachment was also a significant predictor of LCP drug use, with those who have higher levels of parental attachment have expectedly lower levels of LCP drug use. As expected, parental attachment was not effective at reducing LCP offending, which supports Moffitt's (1993) view that LCPs would have weaker social bonds to family.

Consistent with theoretical predictions, higher levels of parental attachment were negatively associated with all 4 outcomes at all 3 waves of data. The parental attachment findings demonstrated a theoretical y consistent relationship with both the offending and drug use outcome variables. This suggests that parental attachment is still a relevant social bond that may act to inhibit criminal behavior for AAOs. This finding is of particular importance as AAOs were conceptualized as older versions of ALs. As Moffitt (1993) described, ALs have stronger social bonds to peers and family. The finding that parental attachment reduces AAO offending supports the idea that AAOs are conceptually similar to ALs and have the same type of background and relationships. The next hypotheses examined the role of economic stability in offending and drug use.

The relationship between economic instability and the outcome variables were clearest in the bivariate analysis, with economic stability being positively correlated with all 4 outcome variables. The multivariate models found that there was a significant relationship between economic instability and the AAO outcome (hypothesis 9), as well as both drug outcomes, with higher levels of economic instability predicting higher levels of AAO offending and AAO and LCP drug use. There were no significant relationships found between economic instability and any of the outcomes using the subsample of "late bloomers" and "persisters."

These findings were consistent with the theoretical predictions of this study, as well as the findings of prior studies. This suggests that economic stability may be utilized as a relevant factor to predict low level offending and drug use. Further, economic instability is important because the economy was one of the areas that has changed the most since the men in the Laub and Sampson's study were young adults. As discussed in chapter 2, the men in Laub and Sampson's sample had a significantly greater likelihood of living a middle class lifestyle than more recent cohorts. Young people today face diminished opportunities and significantly greater levels of economic instability. The findings of this study may provide a foundation for which to study the role of these economic shifts for modern cohorts.

The final turning point theorized to influence AAO offending was property ownership (hypothesis 10). This hypothesis was not supported. However, the relationship between property ownership and offending and drug use had a varied relationship that depended upon the analytic technique. Correlations with the AAO and LCP offending outcomes were negative; however, correlations with the AAO drug use outcome were positive. The negative relationships with AAO and LCP offending were in the expected direction; however, the positive correlation of property ownership with AAO drug use was surprising. Further, owning more property predicted higher rates of AAO drug use, which was the opposite of the relationship theorized. A possible explanation for these findings may be rooted in the low-level substances themselves. Both alcohol and marijuana are much more commonly used in current generations than in past generations. An increase in property ownership means that the individual would have more money and private space that is less likely to be policed or otherwise influenced by formal social controls. In other words, those who own their own homes have greater levels of privacy, and thus are more likely to engage in low-level drug use.

IMPLICATIONS FOR POLICY AND THEORY

As discussed in chapter 1, there are numerous implications of this study for both policy and theory. It should be noted that the influence of many of the turning points and social bonds may not be fully visible until Wave 4 of the data are released. The identification of AAOs may lead to increased pressure on the criminal justice system to process an influx of low-level cases. However, there are particular findings that are of note for policy. The first is the role of education which was found to increase AAO offending. As previously mentioned, this may be due to the typical forms of deviance and alcohol and drug use found on college and university campuses (White et al., 2006).

The presence of AAO's may push many colleges and universities to expand existing disciplinary and support structures, such as disciplinary committees, to deal with low level offending and drug use on campuses. Schools may also have to increase the presence of private security and police forces, increase the level of drug treatment and counseling services offered on campus, and faculty and staff may need to be trained to identify students who are at risk. In other words, colleges and universities may be pushed into caregiver roles more traditionally held by parents and lower level educational facilities (e.g., grade schools and high schools).

Like education, religious participation was found to be related to AAO offending, and AAO and LCP drug use, higher religious participation was related to decreases in AAO offending, and lower use of AAO and LCP drugs. Religious participation may be an important component in reducing offending in AAOs. Programs targeted at emerging adults may want to incorporate a religious component or encourage religious participation to help reduce offending. Further, religious participation was related to reducing both AAO and LCP drug use. As prior studies such as Amoateng and Bahr (1986) and Richard, Bell, and Carlson (2000) have found religious participation is an important component of drug treatment and may act to inhibit drug use. The results of this study supported these findings and as such, may provide a valuable component of successful drug treatment for emerging adults.

Increased parental attachment was found, as with religious participation, to reduce AAO offending, as well as AAO and LCP drug use. This finding is important because it identified the importance of the parental bond in reducing offending during emerging adulthood.

Parental bonds may be a challenge to maintain as many emerging adults "boomerang" (Okimoto & Stegal, 1987) in and out of their parent's homes. However, it is important that diversion programs in which AAOs may be placed try to engage parents. Further, parental involvement may be an essential component of successful drug treatment for emerging adults.

Higher levels of economic instability were found to increase AAO offending, and AAO and LCP drug use. These findings may have several implications for criminal justice policy. As the economic challenges of the last few years continue, we may expect to see an increased amount of low level offenders, and both low and more serious drug users. It is possible that the increased economic stress may be influencing offending and drug use. Many AAOs will most likely be placed in diversion and drug treatment programs. These programs may need to employ financial counseling services to assist AAOs in processing stress and developing strategies to maintain financial well being.

The results of this study found the amount of property owned increased the level of AAO drug use. This finding is of value because it suggests that an increase in the amount of property owned is related to low-level drug use, in this case alcohol and marijuana. From a policy perspective, this presents a challenge. The home is traditionally reserved as private space and is significantly more difficult to police compared to public spaces. Police may need to rely on neighbors to report excessive alcohol use or marijuana use by emerging adults.

As discussed in chapter 1, this study had several possible implications for criminological theory. Recall that Arnett's theory of emerging adulthood focuses on how social changes that have occurred in recent decades have altered the timing of traditional turning points, as well as has the potential to alter social bonds. This study identified the arrested adolescent offender and found support for several hypotheses that may advance criminology theory.

The identification of AAOs and the direct testing of the theory of emerging adulthood have several implications for criminological theory. Identifying AAOs provides an important addition to Moffitt's existing taxonomy, laying a foundation for future studies that may explore the role of AAOs both during emerging adulthood, and as they continue through other stages of the life course. This study also tested many of Laub and Sampson's (2003) turning points and social bonds, finding that many, but not all, were still relevant factors in predicting offending for more modern cohorts. Finally, this study provided (to the author's knowledge) the most extensive test of Arnett's theory of emerging adulthood using criminological data and hypotheses. Next, specific theoretical implications are examined.

Of the demographic factors examined, both age and gender were significantly related to AAO and LCP offending. As expected, as members of the sample age, the rate of offending decreases. This is consistent with Gottfredson and Hirschi's (1990) view that the relationship between age and crime is invariant, and will not vary based on historical context. While the focus of this study was not to test the age-crime curve, it does suggest that emerging adulthood has not yet altered the traditional age-crime curve for either less serious or more serious crime; however, as future waves of the Add Health data become available an effect may be found.

As with age, gender was not the focus of this study. However, as discussed in chapter 3, prior studies dealing with life course theory (e.g., Laub & Sampson, 2003) did not include females in their sample. Further, as many scholars argue (e.g., Belknap, 2007) that female criminality has been overlooked historically. Including gender in these analyses attempted to address these weaknesses. This study found that females have a lower rate of AAO offending. This supported prior studies (e.g., Moffitt et al., 2001) that found female offending peaks earlier in the life course. It also suggests that emerging adulthood has not altered this pattern of offending for females. However, as society continues to progress to more egalitarian gender roles future studies examining offending during emerging adulthood may want to focus on the difference between male and female offending.

Unlike age and gender, race was not a predictor of AAO or LCP offending. However, race was a significant predictor of both AAO and LCP drug use. This finding may be of use to help explain drug use patterns of Black emerging adults, relative to other racial ethnic groups. However, prior research has found that Blacks typically have higher rates of arrest for selling drugs relative to whites (Blumstein, 1995). This study included drug selling as a component of the LCP outcome variable. Future studies may want to compare Blacks and non-Blacks to see if emerging adulthood has altered patterns of arrests for drug offenses.

Having higher levels of education was found to increase both AAO offending and AAO drug use, supporting the findings of prior studies examining offending and drug use during emerging adulthood (e.g.,

White et al., 2006). Scholars have typically found that education influences delinquency and offending with higher levels of education typically reducing offending by increasing social capital (Lochner & Moretti, 2004). However, the results of this study found the opposite, with higher levels of education predicting AAO offending and drug use. As mentioned above, this may be due to the typical forms of deviance and alcohol and drug use found on college and university campuses. This finding is of particular importance as it was in the opposite of the direction expected, and was contrary to a large portion of prior research examining the relationship between education and offending. This finding may imply that education "works" differently for those in emerging adulthood. Due to the extended adolescence that many experience during emerging adulthood, the increase in the rate of college attendance, and the decrease in informal social controls that accompany many of the delayed turning points during emerging adulthood. Future studies may want to conceptualize the role of education during emerging adulthood as *influencing* low level offending and drug use.

As with education, hours worked per week was also a significant predictor of AAO offending, with those who worked more hours having lower levels of offending. This finding was in the predicted direction and supported the results of prior studies examining the role of employment in reducing offending (e.g., Laub & Sampson, 2003). This finding is of value as it provides support for employment continuing to play a role in reducing offending. The remainder of this section will discuss the findings dealing with social bonds and how they influence criminological theory.

Religious participation was found to reduce AAO offending, and both AAO drug use and LCP drug use. This supports the findings of prior studies (e.g., Laub & Sampson, 2001). These findings are of value because research in emerging adulthood has found that emerging adults are less likely to attend religious services (Arnett, 1998). However, this study found that religious participation is still an effective social bond. Life course theorists may want to continue to explore religious participation and its role in reducing offending and drug use for emerging adults, as well as the role of faith-based programs providing treatment for drug offenders.

Economic instability was related to both AAO offending and AAO drug use, with those having higher levels of economic instability having higher rates of both behaviors. This is of importance for criminological theory because future studies may want to consider economic stability as a significant predictor of offending and drug use. The role of economics has been included in prior theoretical discussions (see Wilson, 1987; 1996), but recent economic shifts that have lead to emerging adulthood, as well as the current economic crisis may play a vital role in offending patterns of emerging adults. Life course theory in particular should place greater emphasis on economic well-being, a concept typically discussed in other theoretical arenas such as strain theory. Merton's (1938) theory argued that society places pressure on individuals to accomplish societal goals that few actually have access to the opportunities and means necessary to reach. This places "strain" on individuals, some use crime as a response to this strain and as a way of attaining cultural goals. The pressure to achieve society's (material) goals has increased since Merton first proposed his theory, yet as discussed extensively here, many have a decreased likelihood of living a middle class lifestyle and attaining those goals. Future studies may want to integrate Arnett's theory of emerging adulthood with strain theory due to the economic downturns of the last several years.

Parental attachment was a predictor of both AAO offending and LCP drug use, with higher levels of parental attachment reducing both behaviors. These findings support prior studies (e.g., Hirschi, 1969; Moffitt et al., 2001) and support the hypothesis that bonds with parents are still a valid and important relationship that can reduce offending. Life course theory has focused on the role of social bonds, and in particular bonds to family members such as parents. The findings of this study indicate that theorists should continue to place an emphasis on familial bonds as they explore theoretical explanations of criminal and delinquent behaviors.

The results of this study also have implications for theorists, such as Arnett and Cote, who work in the area of emerging adulthood. The results of this study suggest that economic changes may play an increased role in influencing offending and drug use for emerging adults. Theorists working in emerging adulthood may want to examine the role of economics in influencing risky and dangerous behaviors. Further, several possible protective factors were identified by this study including gender (female), religious participation, and parental bonds. Scholars in the area of emerging adulthood may want to explore the role of these factors in reducing risky, deviant, and criminal behaviors.

Taken as a whole, the findings of this study suggest that emerging adulthood, and more specifically the arrested adolescent offender, have implications for both policy and theory. Criminal justice policies dealing with processing and treatment of offenders may need to be amended to take into account the arrested adolescent offender and their unique needs. Criminological theory, in particular life course theory, has had an addition with the arrested adolescent offender, as well as a more expansive examination of the relationship of emerging adulthood and offending.

STRENGTHS, LIMITATIONS, & AVENUES OF FUTURE RESEARCH

The main strength of this study was that it was able to add a new offender typology that had not been identified in existing taxonomies currently available in the life course literature. The identification of the arrested adolescent offender merged ideas from Moffitt's taxonomy with Arnett's theory of emerging adulthood, producing a strong bond between the life course criminological approach and emerging adulthood. This bond is of particular importance as many of the changes that Arnett identified as causing emerging adulthood have become more prevalent. In addition, many criminologists believe that there may be an upsurge in youth offending which may be influenced by emerging adulthood. The arrested adolescent offender may be able to assist both theorists and practitioners in identifying AAOs and developing strategies to process them.

Criminological examinations of emerging adulthood have been limited in the past. This study took an expansive theoretical and analytical look into this new stage of the life course providing a foundation upon which future researchers can build. Further, it was able to apply Laub and Sampson's age-graded theory of social control to a more recent cohort and using a large sample, finding that many (though not all) of the traditional turning points and social bonds that were relevant for their sample still have value today. This is of particular relevance as Laub and Sampson's work is extremely prevalent in the life course theoretical arena. Further, it is of particular importance that researchers distinguish different types of offenders in order to study how offending patterns may change over time and as offender's progress through the life course.

Another strength of this study was its ability to control for the role of gender and race. Prior studies in life course theory have often been limited to exclusively male, minority, and often offender-only populations. This study used a nationally representative sample and therefore the results may be more generalizable than those of prior studies using smaller samples that were not able to examine the role of race and gender, or only used offender populations.

The major limitation of this study is that while all three waves of data were used to identify the offender typologies, multivariate analyses were limited to a cross sectional design using one wave of data. Recall that emerging adulthood is a relatively recent social phenomenon, and there have been few cohorts that have experienced it. As this sample continues to age and the Add Health study continues, more sophisticated longitudinal designs will be able to be employed to study the long term offending trajectories of the sample.

The utility of several of the indicators of turning points and social bonds were limited due to the age of the sample. The role of job satisfaction, parenthood, marriage, and children may all have been restricted because of the age of the sample. The influence of these turning points and social bonds may become more prevalent as the sample ages.

Another limitation was the inability to fully examine the influence of military service for emerging adults. As previously discussed, data regarding those service in the current Middle East crisis was not available for this study. This prevented this study from being able to examine how modern military service acts (or fails to act) as a turning point.

As with many prior studies the findings of this project answer many questions, but it also bring others to the forefront. One important avenue for future research will be the long term influence of emerging adulthood for the "arrested adolescent" offender and life course persistent offenders. Other areas of interest are the role of the military. Emerging adults will have a higher percentage of their number serve in the Middle East. A future area of inquiry will be how military service "works" for these individuals. A detailed qualitative analysis using a sample of emerging adults would help clarify the role of military service as a turning point for modern cohorts.

Another avenue of future research would be to continue to examine evidence for the construct validity of the AAO. As the sample ages and subsequent waves of the Add Health data are released it would be expected that the prevalence of AAOs would decrease as those who were identified as AAOs at wave 3 reach delayed turning points. In contrast, the prevalence of LCPs in the sample would decline more gradually, with LCPs offending for an longer period of time. As Moffitt discussed, LCPs typically have weaker bonds to conventional society, so it is unlikely that the turning points and social bonds discussed here would have the same influence on LCPs as they would on AAOs. It may not be possible to fully address the role of turning points and social bonds for LCPs and AAOs until the sample is older and a retrospective study could be conducted examining their offending trajectories over the life course.

In closing, the multivariate models found that there were several demographic factors, turning points, and social bonds that were predictive of AAO offending, AAO drug use, and LCP drug use. The findings most relevant for this study are directly related to the AAO outcome. Education, religious participation, hours worked, economic instability, and parental attachment were all significant predictors of AAO offending. These results helped to clarify how traditional turning points and social bonds operate for emerging adults, tie emerging adulthood directly to the life course literature, and lay the foundation for an exciting area of future study. In short, the new stage of emerging adulthood and its implications for identifying AAO offending and offenders appear to be an important area of study.

Description of Outcome Variables and Scales

Wave 1 Adolescent Limited Offending Delinquency Scale	Scale created by summing the following items: In the past 12 months, how often did you…
	paint graffiti or signs on someone else's property or in public place? (0 = never; 1 = once or twice; 2 = three or four times; 3 = five or more times)
	deliberately damage property that didn't belong to you
	lie to parents about whereabouts
	Shoplift
	run away from home
	steal something worth less than $50
	Loud or rowdy in a public place
Wave 2 Adolescent Limited Offending Delinquency Scale	Scale created by summing the following items: In the past 12 months, how often did you…
	paint graffiti or signs on someone else's property or in public place? (0 = never; 1 = once or twice; 2 = three or four times; 3 = five or more times)
	deliberately damage property that didn't belong to you
	lie to parents about whereabouts
	Shoplift
	run away from home
	steal something worth less than $50
	loud or rowdy in a public place

Wave 3 Arrested Adolescent Offending Crime Scale	Scale created by summing the following items: In the past 12 months, how often did you…
	deliberately damage property that didn't belong to you(0 = never; 1 = once or twice; 2 = three or four times; 3 = five or more times)
	steal something worth less than $50
	buy, sell, or hold stolen property
	use someone else's credit card, bank card, or automatic teller card without their permission or knowledge
	deliberately write a bad check
Wave 1 Life Course Persistent Offending Delinquency/Crime Scale	Scale created by summing the following items: In the past 12 months, how often did you…
	hurt someone badly enough to need bandages or care from a doctor or nurse (0 = never; 1 = once or twice; 2 = three or four times; 3 = five or more times)
	drive a car without owner's permission
	go into a house or building to steal something
	use or threaten to use a weapon to get something from someone
	sell marijuana or other drugs
	take part in a fight where a group of your friends was against another group
	steal something worth more than $50
Wave 2 Life Course Persistent Offending Delinquency/Crime Scale	Scale created by summing the following items: In the past 12 months, how often did you…
	drive a car without owner's permission(0 = never; 1 = once or twice; 2 = three or four times; 3 = five or more times)
	go into a house or building to steal something
	use or threaten to use a weapon to get something from someone
	sell marijuana or other drugs
	take part in a fight where a group of your friends was against another group
	steal something worth more than $50
	initiated into a gang

Wave 3 Life Course Persistent Offending Crime Scale	Scale created by summing the following items: In the past 12 months, how often did you…
	steal something worth more than $50 (0 = never; 1 = once or twice; 2 = three or four times; 3 = five or more times)
	go into a house or building to steal something
	use or threaten to use a weapon to get something from someone
	sell marijuana or other drugs
	take part in a fight where a group of your friends was against another group
	use a weapon in a fight
	carry a handgun to work or school
Wave 1 Adolescent Limited Drug Use Scale	Scale created by summing the following items from Wave 1:
	Have you ever tried smoking, even just 1 or 2 puffs? (0 = no; 1 = yes)
	Have you ever had a drink of beer, wine, or liquor – not just a sip or a taste of someone else's drink – more than 2 or 3 times in your life? (0 = no; 1 = yes)
	How old were you when you tried marijuana for the first time? (0 = no; 1 = yes)
Wave 2 Adolescent Limited Drug Use Scale	Scale created by summing the following items from Wave 2:
	Have you ever tried smoking, even just 1 or 2 puffs? (0 = no; 1 = yes)
	Have you ever had a drink of beer, wine, or liquor – not just a sip or a taste of someone else's drink – more than 2 or 3 times in your life? (0 = no; 1 = yes)
	How old were you when you tried marijuana for the first time? (0 = no; 1 = yes)

Wave 3 Arrested Adolescent Drug Use Scale	Scale created by summing the following items from Wave 3:
	Have you ever tried smoking, even just 1 or 2 puffs? (0 = no; 1 = yes)
	Have you ever had a drink of beer, wine, or liquor – not just a sip or a taste of someone else's drink – more than 2 or 3 times in your life? (0 = no; 1 = yes)
	How old were you when you tried marijuana for the first time? (0 = no; 1 = yes)
Wave 1 Life Course Persistent Offender Drug Use Scale	Scale created by summing the following items from Wave 1:
	How old were you when you tried any kind of cocaine – including power, freebase, or crack cocaine If you never tried cocaine enter "0." (0 = no; 1 = yes)
	How old were you when you tried inhalants, such as glue or solvents, for the first time? If you never tried inhalants, such as these enter "0." (0 = no; 1 = yes)
	How old were you when you first tried any other type of illegal drug, such as LSD, PCP, ecstasy, mushrooms, speed, ice, heroin or pills, without a doctor's prescription. If you never tried any illegal drug enter "0." (0 = no; 1 = yes)
Wave 2 Life Course Persistent Offender Drug Use Scale	Scale created by summing the following items from Wave 2: Since last interview....(0 = no; 1 = yes)
	have you tried or used any kind of cocaine – including powder, freebase, or crack cocaine?
	have you tried inhalants, such as glue or solvents
	have you tried or used any other type of illegal drug, such as LSD, PCP, ecstasy, mushrooms, speed, ice, heroin or pills, without a doctor's prescription?
Wave 3 Life Course Persistent Offender Drug Use Scale	Scale created by summing the following items from Wave 3: Since June 1995 have you....(0 = no; 1 = yes)
	used any kind of cocaine including-crack, freebase, or powder?
	used any other types of illegal drugs such as LSD, PCP, ecstasy, mushrooms, inhalants, ice, heroin, or prescription medicines, not prescribed for you?

Description of Independent Variables Scales

Wave1 Education Attachment Scale	Scale create by summing the following items from wave 1:
	You feel close to people at your school? (1 = strongly disagree; 2 = disagree; 3 = neither agree, nor disagree; 4 = agree; 5 = strongly agree)
	You feel like you are part of your school?
	You are happy to be at school?
Wave 1 Employment Scale	Scale create by summing the following items from wave 1:
	How many hours per week do your work in the summer?
	How many hours per week do you work non-summer?
Wave 1 Low Self Control Scale	Scale created by summing the following items from wave 1:
	How often do you have getting along with your teachers? (0 = never; 1 = just a few times; 2 = about once a week; 3 = almost every day; 4 = everyday
	How often do you have trouble paying attention?
	How often do you have difficulty finishing your homework?
Wave1 Parental Attachment Scale	Scale created by summing the following items from wave 1:
	How close do you feel with your mother? (1 = not at all; 2 = very little; 3 = somewhat; 4 = quite a bit; 5 = very much)
	How close do you feel with your father?
	How much does mom care?
	How much does dad care?

Wave 2 **Education Attachment Scale**	Scale create by summing the following items from wave 1:
	You feel close to people at your school? (1 = strongly disagree; 2 = disagree; 3 = neither agree, nor disagree; 4 = agree; 5 = strongly agree) You feel like you are part of your school? You are happy to be at school?
Wave 2 **Employment Scale**	Scale create by summing the following items from wave 2:
	How many hours per week do your work in the summer? How many hours per week do you work non-summer?
Wave 2 **Low Self Control Scale**	Scale created by summing the following items from wave 2:
	How often do you have getting along with your teachers? (0 = never; 1 = just a few times; 2 = about once a week; 3 = almost every day; 4 = everyday) How often do you have trouble paying attention? How often do you have difficulty finishing your homework?
Wave 2 **Parental Attachment Scale**	Scale created by summing the following items from wave 2:
	How close do you feel with your mother? (1 = not at all; 2 = very little; 3 = somewhat; 4 = quite a bit; 5 = very much) How close do you feel with your father? How much does mom care? How much does dad care?
Wave 3 **Economic Well Being Scale**	In the past 12 months was there a time when (0 = no; 1 = yes)
	...you were without telephone service because you did not have enough money to pay the bill? …you did not have enough money to pay the full amount of rent or mortgage? …were evicted from house/apartment for not paying rent or mortgage? …did not pay the full amount of gas, electric, or oil company would not deliver? …did not go to see a doctor or go to the hospital because you could not pay the bill?

Wave 3 Parental Attachment Scale	Scale created by summing the following items from wave 3:
	How close do you feel with your mother? (1 = not at all; 2 = very little; 3 = somewhat; 4 = quite a bit; 5 = very much) How close do you feel with your father?
Wave 3 Property Owned Scale	Scale created by summing the following items from wave 3:
	Do you own the following items (0 = no; 1 = yes) …a residence (house, condo, or mobile home)? …a motor vehicle (car, truck, or motorcycle)? …a computer? Do you have one of the following (0 = no; 1 = yes) …a checking account? …a credit card?

Controlling Alpha Inflation

Conducting analyses with multiple dependent variables that are correlated increases the possibility of a Type I error occurring. In other words, using multiple correlated dependent variables is likely to find a significant relationship with some of the independent variables by chance. The probability of Type I error can be calculated as:

$$\text{Probability of Type I error} = 1 - (1-\alpha)^n$$

For example, if 10 analyses were conducted with the standard alpha level of p<.05 the likelihood of finding a false positive would be 1-(1-.05),[10] or 40% (Wilkinson, 1951). One of the most common methods of addressing this issue is a Bonferroni correction (Moran, 2003). The Bonferroni adjustment addresses Type I error by dividing α by the number of statistical tests or $\alpha_\beta = \alpha/n$. Here α_β would be the Bonferroni adjusted alpha level, α is the original alpha level (usually p <.05), and n, the number of statistical tests (Darlington, 1990). For example, employing a Bonferroni adjustment to the above example with 10 tests with a p<.05 alpha level, would results in an alpha level of p<.005 for the final analysis. Some researchers have argued that using a Bonferroni adjustment is overly conservative and may prevent detailed analyses (Moran, 2003). Further, others have stated that Bonferonni adjustments cannot guarantee more accurate results (Perneger, 1998).

The ideal solution to the alpha issue would be a balance between statistical power with issues of statistical sensitivity to finding results. For this study these two competing issues are considered in light of several issues. First, the primary sets of hypotheses are focused on the AAO outcome. These are the core focus of this study and will not be affected by the Bonferroni adjustment. Second, the original levels of significance for the subsequent analyses were largely not impacted by the Bonferroni adjustment. As a result, it was decided to take a conservative approach and employ a Bonferroni adjustment.

Correlational Analyses

Table 23. *Wave 1 Correlations Between Independent Variables and Outcome Variables*

	AL Offending Scale	LCP Offending Scale	AL Drug Use Scale	LCP Drug Use Scale
Age	.097**	.044**	.255**	.063**
Attendance at Religious Services	.050**	.013	.084**	.022
Grade in School	.116**	.015	.262**	.063**
Hours Worked Scale	.100**	.069**	.203**	.070**
Low – Self Control Scale	.389**	.317**	.332**	.201**
Parental Attachment Scale	-.183**	-.159**	-.217**	-.103**
PPVT Score	.054**	-.096**	.006	.034*
School Attachment Scale	-.180**	-.155**	-.208**	-.146**

*=p<.05, **=p<.01

The results of the correlational analysis revealed that all of the continuous independent variables have significant relationships with the adolescent limited offending scale. Beginning with age, there was a significant correlation between the two variables ($r = .097$, $n = 4519$, p

< .01), with those who were older scoring higher on levels of low-level offending. There was a weak positive correlations between attendance at religious services and the AL offense scale variables (r = .050, n = 4519, p < .01), indicating that participation in religious services is associated with increase low-level offending. A small, positive correlation was found between grade in school and the adolescent limited offending scale being explored (r = .116, n = 4519, p < .01), with higher grade levels associated with higher scores on the AL offense scale. There was also a small, positive correlation found between the hours worked per week scale and the adolescent limited offending scale (r = .100, n = 4519, p < .01), with higher scores on the hours worked per week scale associated with higher scores on the adolescent limited offense scale. A medium, positive correlation was found between the low self control scale and the adolescent limited offense scale (r = .389, n = 4519, p < .01), with those who have greater levels of low self control scoring higher on the adolescent limited offense scale. There was a small, negative correlation found between the parental attachment scale and the adolescent limited offending scale (r = -.183, n = 4519, p < .01), indicating that those who score higher on parental attachment have lower levels of adolescent limited offenses. A weak, positive correlation was found between the PPVT score and the adolescent limited offending scale (r = .054, n = 4519, p < .01), with those scoring higher on the PPVT having higher scores on the adolescent limited offending scale. The final relationship examined was between the school attachment scale and the adolescent limited offending scale, a small, negative relationship was found (r = -.180, n = 4519, p < .01), with those scoring higher on school attachment having lower levels of adolescent limited offending.

Correlational analysis revealed that several of the continuous independent variables have significant relationships with the life course persistent offending scale. Starting with age, there was a weak, significant correlation between the two variables (r = .044, n = 4514, p < .01) with those who were older scoring higher on levels of more serious offending. There was also a small, positive correlation found between the hours worked per week scale and the life course persistent offending scale (r = .069, n = 4514, p < .01), with higher scores on the hours worked per week scale associated with higher scores on the life course persistent offending scale. A medium, positive correlation was found between the low self-control scale and the life course persistent offending scale (r = .317, n = 4514, p < .01), with those who have greater levels of low self-control scoring higher on the life course persistent offending scale. There was a small, negative correlation found between the parental attachment scale and the life course persistent offending scale (r = -.159, n = 4514, p < .01), indicating that those who score higher on parental attachment have lower levels of life course persistent offenses. A weak, negative correlation was found between the PPVT score and the life course persistent offending scale (r = -.096, n = 4514, p < .01), with those scoring higher on the PPVT having lower scores on the life course persistent offending scale. The final relationship examined was between the school attachment scale and the life course persistent offending scale, a small, negative relationship was found (r = -.155, n = 4514, p < .01), with those scoring higher on school attachment having lower levels of more serious offending.

The results of the correlational analysis found several of the continuous independent variables have significant relationships with the Adolescent Limited drug use scale. Starting with age, there was a weak, significant correlation between the two variables (r = .255, n = 4519, p < .01) with those who were older scoring higher on lower level drug use. There was a weak positive correlation between attendance at religious services and the AL drugs use scale variable (r = .084, n = 4519, p < .01), indicating that participation in religious services is associated with an increase low-level drug use. A small, positive correlation was found between grade in school and the adolescent limited offending drug use scale (r = .262, n = 4519, p < .01), with higher grade levels associated with higher scores on the AL drug use scale. There was also a small, positive correlation found between the hours worked per week scale and the adolescent limited drug use scale (r = .203, n = 4519, p < .01), with higher scores on the hours worked per week scale associated with higher scores on the adolescent drug use scale. A medium, positive correlation was found between the low self-control scale and the adolescent limited drug use scale (r = .332, n = 4519, p < .01), with those who have greater levels of low self-control scoring higher on the adolescent limited drug use scale. There was a small, negative correlation found between the parental attachment scale and the adolescent limited drug scale (r = -.217, n = 4519, p < .01), indicating that those who score higher on parental attachment have lower levels of adolescent limited drug use. The final relationship examined was between the school attachment scale and the adolescent limited drugs used scale, a small, negative relationship was found (r = -

.208, *n* = 4519, *p* < .01), with those scoring higher on school attachment having lower levels of adolescent limited drug use.

The results of the correlational analysis revealed that several of the continuous independent variables have significant relationships with the life course persistent drug use scale. Starting with age, there was a weak, significant correlation between the two variables (*r* = .063, *n* = 4496, *p* < .01) with those who were older scoring higher on levels of more serious drug use. A small, positive correlation was found between grade in school and the LCP drug use scale (*r* = .063, *n* = 4496, *p* < .01), with higher grade levels associated with higher scores on the LCP drug use scale. There was also a small, positive correlation found between the hours worked per week scale and the LCP drug use scale (*r* = .070, *n* = 4496, *p* < .01), with higher scores on the hours worked per week scale associated with higher scores on the life course persistent drug use scale. A small, positive correlation was found between the low self-control scale and the life course persistent drug use scale (*r* = .201, *n* = 4496, *p* < .01), with those who have greater levels of low self-control scoring higher on the LCP drug use scale. There was a small, negative correlation found between the parental attachment scale and the life course persistent drug use (*r* = -.103, *n* = 4496, *p* < .01), indicating that those who score higher on parental attachment have lower levels of life course persistent drug use. A weak, positive correlation was found between the PPVT score and the life course persistent drug use scale (*r* = .034, *n* = 449, *p* < .05), with those scoring higher on the PPVT having increased scores on the life course persistent drug use scale. The final relationship examined was between the school attachment scale and the life course persistent drug use scale, a small, negative relationship was found (*r* = -.146, *n* = 4496, *p* < .01), with those scoring higher on school attachment having lower levels of more serious drug use. The correlational analyses conducted at wave 2 tested for multicollinearity, and examined the relationships between the continuous independent variables and the outcome variables (see Table 21).

Table 24.   *Wave 2 Correlations Between Independent Variables and Outcome Variables*

	AL Offending Scale	LCP Offending Scale	AL Drug Use Scale	LCP Drug Use Scale
Age	-.019	.007	.146**	.039**
Attendance at Religious Services	-.080**	-.071**	-.158**	-.090**
Grade in School	-.002	-.026	.150**	.042**
Hours Worked Scale	.021	.047**	.165**	.058**
Low – Self Control Scale	.348**	.243**	.278**	.137**
Parental Attachment Scale	-.115**	-.115**	-.128**	-.054**
School Attachment Scale	-.119**	-.101	-.129**	-.103**

*=p<.05, **=p<.01

The results of the correlational analyses revealed that several of the continuous independent variables have significant relationships with the adolescent limited offending scale at wave 2. Beginning with attendance at religious services, there was a significant, weak, negative correlation between the two variables ($r = -.080$, $n = 4555$, $p < .01$) with those who have higher levels of religious participation scoring lower on levels on the adolescent limited offending scale. There was a significant, medium, positive correlation between the score on the low – self control scale and AL offending ($r = -.348$, $n = 4555$, $p < .01$), indicating that those who have less self control will score higher on the AL offense scale. There was a small, negative correlation between the parental attachment scale and the low – level offense scale, $r = -.115$, $n = 4555$, $p < .01$) with those who have stronger attachments to parents scoring lower on the low – level offense scale. The final significant relationship revealed by correlations was between school attachment and the AL offense scale. A weak, negative relationship was found, $r = $

-.119, n = 4555, p < .01)with those scoring higher on school attachment having lower levels of AL offenses.

The results of the correlational analysis found several of the continuous independent variables have significant relationships with the life course persistent offending scale at wave 2. Beginning with attendance at religious services, there was a significant, weak, negative correlation between the two variables (r = -.071, n = 4554, p < .01) with those who have higher levels of religious participation scoring lower on levels on the life course persistent offending scale. There was a small, positive correlation between the hours worked per week scale and the LCP offending scale, (r = .047, n = 4554, p < .01), with those who work more hours having higher scores on the LCP offending scale. A weak, negative correlation was found between the school attachment scale and the LCP offending scale, (r = -.101, n = 4554, p < .01), with those having higher levels of school attachment having lower levels of life course persistent offending at wave 2. A small, positive relationship was found been the low – self control scale and the LCP offending scale, (r = .243, n = 4554, p < .01), with those having higher levels of low-self control scoring higher on the life course persistent offending scale. The final independent variable that had a significant relationship with the LCP offending scale was the parental attachment scale, (r = -.115, n = 4554 p < .01), with the correlation matrix revealing a small, negative relationship, with those scoring higher on the parental attachment scale having lower scores on the LCP offense scale.

The results of the correlational analysis revealed that all of the continuous independent variables have significant relationships with the adolescent limited drugs used scale. Beginning with age, there was a small, positive relationship, (r = .146, n = 4555, p < .01), with those who were older having higher scores on the adolescent limited drug use scale. There was a weak, negative relationship between attendance at religious services and the AL drug use scale, (r = -.158, n = 4555, p < .01), with higher levels of religious participation being associated with a reduction in AL drug use. A small, positive correlation was found between current grade in school and adolescent limited drug use, (r = .150, n = 4555, p < .01), with those in higher grades having increased levels of AL drug use. There was a small, positive relationship found between the score on the hours worked per week scale and the adolescent limited drugs used scale, (r = .165, n = 4555 p < .01), with those scoring higher on the hours worked per week scale having higher scores on the adolescent limited drugs used scale. A small, positive relationship was found between the low – self-control scale and the AL drug use scale, ($r = .278$, $n = 4555$ $p < .01$), with higher levels of low-self-control being positively associated with the score on the AL drugs used scale. There was a small, negative correlation found between the parental attachment scale and the adolescent limited drug use scale, ($r = -.128$, $n = 4555$, $p < .01$), with those who have higher levels of parental attachment scoring lower on the adolescent limited drug use scale. There was a weak, significant relationship found between school attachment and AL drug use, ($r = -.129$, $n = 4555$, $p < .01$).

The results of the correlational analysis revealed that all of the continuous independent variables have significant relationships with the life course persistent drugs used scale. Beginning with age, there was a small, positive relationship, ($r = .039$, $n = 4550$, $p < .01$), with those who were older having higher scores on the life course persistent drug use scale. There was a weak, negative relationship between attendance at religious services and the LCP drug use scale, ($r = -.090$, $n = 4550$, $p < .01$), with higher levels of religious participation being associated with a reduction in LCP drug use. A small, positive correlation was found between current grade in school and the more serious drug use, ($r = .042$, $n = 4550$, $p < .01$), with those in higher grades having increased levels of more serious drug use. There was a small, positive relationship found between the score on the hours worked per week scale and the life course persistent drug use scale, ($r = .058$, $n = 4550$, $p < .01$), with those scoring higher on the hours worked per week scale having higher scores on the life course persistent drug use scale. A small, positive relationship was found between the low – self control scale and the LCP drug use scale, ($r = .137$, $n = 4550$ $p < .01$), with higher levels of low- self control being positively associated with the score on the LCP drug use scale. There was a small, negative correlation found between the parental attachment scale and the life course persistent drug use scale, ($r = -.054$, $n = 4550$, $p < .01$), with those who have higher levels of parental attachment scoring lower on the life course persistent drug use scale. There was a weak, significant relationship found between school attachment and LCP drug use, ($r = -.103$, $n = 4550$, $p < .01$). The final correlational analyses conducted were at wave 3. These analyses are of particular interest, as they are conducted when the sample is in emerging adulthood. These analyses tested for multicollinearity, and provide an examination of the bivariate relationships between the independent and dependent variables at wave 3.

Table 25. *Wave 3 Correlations Between Independent Variables and Outcome Variables*

	AAO Offending Scale	LCP Offending Scale	AAO Drug Use Scale	LCP Drug Use Scale
Age	-.079**	-.091**	-.002	-.020
Attendance at Religious Services	-.078**	-.122**	-.203**	.167**
Current Job Satisfaction	-.028	-.038**	-.029*	-.036*
Economic Well Being Scale	.094**	.078**	.056**	.057**
Highest Grade Completed	-.014	-.111**	.033*	-.028
Hours Worked Scale	-.024	.003	.028	-.007
Parental Attachment Scale	-.063**	-.075**	-.066**	.058**
Property Owned Scale	-.059**	-.119**	.041**	-.024

*=p<.05, **=p<.01

The results of the correlation analysis revealed that several of the continuous independent variables have significant relationships with the arrested adolescent offending scale. Beginning with age, there was a small significant, negative correlation between the two variables ($r = -.079$, $n = 4798$, $p < .01$), with those who were older scoring lower on levels of low-level offending. There was a weak significant, negative correlation between attendance at religious services and the AAO offense scale variables ($r = -.078$, $n = 4798$, $p < .01$), indicating that participation in religious services are associated with decrease in low-level offending. A small, positive correlation was found between the score on the economic well being scale (recall that it is reverse scored, with higher scored indicating lower levels of economic stability) and the arrested adolescent offending scale ($r = .094$, $n = 4798$, $p < .01$), with higher scores on the economic well being score associated with higher scores on the AAO offense scale. There was a small, negative correlation found between the parental attachment scale and the arrested adolescent offending scale ($r = -.063$, $n = 4798$, $p < .01$), indicating that those who score higher on parental attachment have lower levels of arrested adolescent offenses. The final relationship examined was between the property owned scale and the arrested adolescent offending scale, a small, negative relationship was found ($r = -.059$, $n = 4798$, $p < .01$), with those scoring higher on property owned having lower levels of arrested adolescent offending.

The results of the correlational analysis revealed that several of the continuous independent variables have significant relationships with the life course persistent offending scale at wave 2. Beginning with age, there was a significant, weak, negative correlation between the two variables ($r = -.091$, $n = 4800$, $p < .01$) with those who were older scoring lower on levels on the life course persistent offending scale. There was a small, negative correlation between attendance at religious services and the LCP offending scale, ($r = -.122$, $n = 4800$, $p < .01$), with those who work attend religious services more often having lower scores on the LCP offending scale. A weak, negative correlations was found between current job satisfaction and the LCP offending scale, ($r = -.038$, $n = 4800$, $p < .01$), with those having higher levels job satisfaction having lower levels of life course persistent offending at wave 3. A small, positive relationship was found been the economic well being scale and the LCP offending scale, ($r = .078$, $n = 4800$, p $<$ .01), with those having higher levels of economic instability scoring higher on the life course persistent offending scale. A small significant, negative correlation was found between the highest grade completed and the LCP offending scale, ($r = -.111$, $n = 4800$, $p < .01$), with those with higher levels of education scoring low on the serious offending scale. A minor significant, negative relationship was found between the parental attachment scale and the LCP offending scale, ($r = -.075$, $n = 4800$, $p < .01$), with those who have stronger attachments to parents having lower levels of LCP offending. The final independent variable that had a significant relationship with the LCP offending scale was the property owned scale, ($r = -.119$, $n = 480$ $p < .01$), with the correlation matrix revealing a small, negative relationship, with those scoring higher on the property owned scale having lower scores on the LCP offense scale.

The results of the correlational analysis revealed that all of the continuous independent variables have significant relationships with the arrested adolescent drugs used scale. Beginning with age, attendance at religious services and the AAO drugs used scale, there was a small significant, positive relationship (r = -.203, n = 4803, $p <$ .01), with higher levels of religious participation being associated with a reduction in AAO drug use. A small significant, negative relationship was found between current job satisfaction and arrested adolescent drug use, (r = -.029, n = 4803, $p <$ .05), with those who have lower levels of job satisfaction scoring higher on the AAO drug use scale. A small significant, positive relationship was found between economic well being and the AAO drug use, (r = .056, n = 4803, $p <$ .01), with those who have higher levels of economic insatiability scoring higher on the AAO drug use scale. A small, positive correlation was found between level of education and arrested adolescent drugs used, (r = .033 n = 4803, $p <$ .05), with those in higher grades having increased levels of AAO drug use. There was a small, negative correlation found between the parental attachment scale and the arrested adolescent drug use scale, (r = -.066, n = 4803, $p <$ .01), with those who have higher levels of parental attachment scoring lower on the arrested adolescent drug use scale. There was a weak significant, positive relationship found between property owned and AAO drug use, (r = .041, n = 4803, $p <$ .01).

The results of the correlational analysis revealed that all of the continuous independent variables have significant relationships with the life course persistent drug used scale. Beginning with attendance at religious services, there was a small significant, negative relationship, (r = -.167, n = 4765, $p <$ .01), with higher levels of religious participation being associated with a reduction in LCP drug use. A minor, positive correlation was found between current job satisfaction and LCP drug use , (r = -.036, n = 4765, $p <$ .05), with those who have higher levels of job satisfaction scoring lower on the LCP drug use scale. A small, positive correlation was found between the economic well being scale and the more serious drugs used, (r = .057, n = 4765, p < .01), with those who had higher levels of economic instability having increased levels of more serious drug use. There was a small, negative correlation found between the parental attachment scale and the life course persistent drug use scale, (r = -.058, n = 4765, $p <$ .01), with those who have higher levels of parental attachment scoring lower on the life course persistent drug use scale.

Late Bloomer & Persisters Analyses

These series of models looks at the unique effect of the demographic variables, indicators or turning points, and social bond measures on a sub-sample of the population identified as "late bloomers." This sub-sample consists of members of the sample who were not active offenders at wave 2 of the Add Health data. This sub-population of "late bloomers" became active during wave 3 of the data. There were 200 "late bloomers" identified within the sample. Due to the small sample, analyses were conducted using three separate models (demographics, turning points, and social bonds) that do not control for the other factors. While there is no generalizable answer or guidelines for the required sample size needed per each predictor in a regression model (e.g, Stevens, 1996) recommended 15 subjects per predictor, Pallant (2007) recommends 40 subjects per predictor depending on the type of regression) it was decided to take a conservative approach and run individual models with each set of predictors. The first series of models examines the influence of demographic factors, turning points, and social bonds in predicted AAO offending for the subsample of "late bloomers." To minimize the risk of alpha inflation a Bonferroni correction, of p<.025 was employed for this series of models.

Table 26.   *Negative Binomial Regression Models of Late Bloomers on Independent Variables and AAO Outcome*

AAO Offending Scale	Model 1			Model 2			Model 3		
	B	(SE)	IRR	B	(SE)	IRR	B	(SE)	IRR
Age	-.056	.060	.945						
Gender	-.363	.233	.694						
Black	.369	.361	1.44						
White	.362	.292	1.43						
Military				.237	1.06	1.27			
Children				.317	.249	1.37			
Education				.073	.061	1.07			
Hours Worked				-.010	.011	.989			
Married				-.171	.502	.842			
Religious Services							-.162	.069	.850*
Economic Instability							-.259	.194	.772
Job Satisfaction							-.113	.129	.893
Parental Attachment							-.040	.105	.961
Property Owned [1]							.319	.198	1.38
Constant	.757	1.30		-.921	.954		.429	.515	

*p<.05   Chi – Square = 4.81   Chi – Square = 3.90   Chi – Square = 11.13

**p<.01   Df = 4   Df = 5   Df = 5

Log likelihood = -.243.02   Log likelihood = -243.48   Log likelihood = -239.87

AIC = 2.47   AIC = 2.49   AIC = 2.46

The economic instability, parental attachment, and property owned scales were z scored and mean summed.

Demographics

Model 1 included only the demographic variables being controlled for in the analysis. None of the demographic variables were significant in this model. However, it is worth noting that while not significant, the relationships between the demographic variables and the AAO outcome were in the expected directions. Age had a negative relationship, suggesting that older offenders would offend less. Gender was also negative, suggesting females would have had lower incidences of AAO offenses. Blacks, as compared to other groups, would have had lower rate of AAO offending. Whites, compared to other groups, would have had a lower incident rate of AAO offenses.

Turning Points

Indicators of traditional turning points were included into the next model. Of the indicators added, none were significant. While none of the turning point indicators were significant, some were not in the predicted direction. Those who were actively serving in the military would have had higher rates of AAO offending, as would those who had children. Those who were married would have had lower levels of AAO offending, as would have those with higher levels of education, and those who worked more hours.

Social Bonds

Indicators of social bonds were included in model 3. Religious participation was the only variable that was significant, for every one unit increase in religious participation there was a 15% decrease in AAO offending, holding constant all other variables in the model ($p<.05$, IRR = .850). The next series of models explored the influence of the demographic variables, turning points, and social bonds on the LCP outcome (see Table 24).

Table 27. *Negative Binomial Regression Models of Late Bloomers on Independent Variables and LCP Outcome*

LCP Offending Scale	Model 1			Model 2			Model 3		
	B	(SE)	IRR	B	(SE)	IRR	B	(SE)	IRR
Age	-.022	.035	.978						
Gender	-.046	.131	.954						
Black	.009	.201	1.01						
White	.007	.160	1.01						
Military				-.173	.719	.841			
Children				-.002	.150	.998			
Education				-.013	.035	.987			
Hours Worked				.001	.006	1.01			
Married				-.180	.281	.835			
Religious Services							-.017	.037	.983
Economic Instability[1]							.006	.091	1.01
Job Satisfaction							.004	.075	1.00
Parental Attachment[1]							-.011	.061	.989
Property Owned[1]							-.075	.111	.928
Constant	.718	.747		.408	.533		.249	.306	
*p<.05	Chi – Square = .51			Chi – Square = .67			Chi – Square = .97		
**p<.01	Df = 4			Df = 5			Df = 5		
	Log likelihood = -234.46			Log likelihood = 234.38			Log likelihood = -234.27		
	AIC = 2.36			AIC = 2.37			AIC = 2.37		

Demographics

Model 1 included only the demographic variables being controlled for in the analysis. None of the demographic variables were significant in this model. However, it is worth noting that while not significant, the relationships between the demographic variables and the LCP outcome were in the expected directions. Age had a negative relationship, suggesting that older offenders would offend less. Gender was also negative, suggesting females would have had lower incidences of LCP offenses. Blacks, as compared to other groups, would have had lower rate of LCP offending. Whites, compared to other groups, would also have had a lower incident rate of LCP offenses.

Turning Points

Indicators of traditional turning points were included into the next model. Of the indicators added, none were significant. While none of the turning point indicators were significant, all went in the predicted direction. Those who were actively serving in the military would have had lower rates of LCP offending, as would those who had children, those who were married, those with higher levels of education, and those who worked more hours.

Social Bonds

Indicators of social bonds were included in model 3. As with the first 2 models none of the indicators of social bonds were significant. Despite the lack of significance, the direction of the relationship still provides an indication of the possible relationships that exist between these variables and LCP offenses. All of the variables were in the predicted direction, having more property owned, stronger bonds with parents, greater levels of religious participation and job satisfaction all would have reduced LCP offenses, if significant. The economic stability variable (reverse scored) was also in the predicted direction, with those having higher levels of instability having greater levels of LCP offenses (if significant). The next series of models examined the role of demographics, social bonds, and turning points in predicting AAO drug use (see Table 25).

Table 28.   *Poisson Regression Models of Late Bloomers on AAO Drug Use Outcome*

AAO Drug Use Scale	Model 1			Model 2			Model 3		
	B	(SE)	IRR	B	(SE)	IRR	B	(SE)	IRR
Age	-.004	.025	.996						
Gender	-.056	.097	.945						
Black	-.225	.157	.797						
White	.042	.117	1.04						
Military				-.137	.509	.872			
Children				-.034	.113	.966			
Education				-.001	.025	.999			
Hours Worked				.004	.005	1.01			
Married				-.082	.207	.920			
Religious Services							-.049	.028	.952
Economic Instability[1]							-.038	.072	.963
Job Satisfaction							-.015	.055	.984
Parental Attachment [1]							-.016	.045	.984
Property Owned [1]							-.105	.084	1.11
*p<.05	Chi – Square = 5.28			Chi – Square = 1.06			Chi – Square = 5.13		
**p<.01	Df = 4			Df = 5			Df = 5		
	Log likelihood = - 308.33			Log likelihood = - 310.45			Log likelihood = -308.41		
	AIC = 3.12			AIC = 3.14			AIC = 3.12		

The economic instability, parental attachment, and property owned scales were z scored and mean summed.

Poisson regression models were used because of the over dispersion in AAO drug use outcome variable (Long & Freese, 2006; StataCorp, 2006). Three separate models were completed. Model one included demographic variables, age, gender, and two dummy variables capturing the unique effect of race. Model 2 looked at the effects of turning points on the amount low level drugs used. Model 3 examined social bonds.

Demographics

Model 1 included only the demographic variables being controlled for in the analysis. None of the demographic variables were significant in this model. However, it is worth noting that while not significant, the relationships between the demographic variables and the AAO drug use outcome were in the expected directions. Age had a negative relationship, suggesting that older offenders would offend less. Gender was also negative, suggesting females would have lower incidences of AAO drug use. Blacks, as compared to other groups, would have had lower rate of AAO offending. In contrast, whites, compared to other groups, would have had a higher incident rate of AAO drug use.

Turning Points

Indicators of traditional turning points were included into the next model. Of the indicators added, none were significant. While none of the turning point indicators were significant, all went in the predicted direction. Those who were actively serving in the military would have had lower rates of AAO drug use, as would those who had children, those who were married, those with higher levels of education, and those who worked more hours.

Social Bonds

Indicators of social bonds were included in model 3. As with the first 2 models none of the indicators of social bonds were significant. Despite the lack of significance, the direction of the relationship still provides an indication of the possible relationships that exist between these variables and AAO drug use. All of the variables were in the predicted direction, having more property owned, stronger bonds with parents, greater levels of religious participation and job satisfaction all would have reduced AAO drug use, if significant. The economic stability variable (reverse scored) was also in the predicted direction, with those having higher levels of instability having greater levels of AAO drug use (if significant). The final model examining "late bloomers" explored the influence of demographic factors, turning points, and social bonds in predicted LCP drug use (Table 26).

Table 29. *Negative Binomial Regression Models of Late Bloomers on LCP Drug Use Outcome*

LCP Drug Used Scale	Model 1			Model 2			Model 3		
	B	(SE)	IRR	B	(SE)	IRR	B	(SE)	IRR
Age	.086	.054	1.09						
Gender	-.154	.226	.857						
Black	-2.02	.751	.131*						
White	.456	.275	1.58						
Military				1.13	.836	3.09			
Children				-.460	.287	.631			
Education				-.089	.059	.914			
Hours Worked				-.008	.011	.992			
Married				-.722	.621	.485			
Religious Services							-.241	.075	.786**
Economic Instability							.078	.146	1.08
Job Satisfaction							-.070	.122	.933
Parental Attachment							-.116	.098	.890
Property Owned							.158	.189	1.17
Constant	-2.69	1.20					-151	.484	
*p<.05	Chi – Square = 31.49			Chi – Square = 7.93			Chi – Square = 13.95		
**p<.01	Df = 4			Df = 5			Df = 5		
	Log likelihood = -168.46			Log likelihood = -180.24			Log likelihood = -177.23		
	AIC = 1.74			AIC = 1.87			AIC = 1.84		

The economic instability, parental attachment, and property owned scales were z scored and mean summed.

Demographics

Model 1 included only the demographic variables being controlled for in the analysis. The only demographic variable that was significant was Black, with Blacks, as compared to other groups having an 86% lower incident rate of LCP drug use, holding constant all other variables in the model (p<.01, IRR = .132).

Turning Points

Indicators of traditional turning points were included into the next model. Of the indicators added, none were significant. While none of the turning point indicators were significant, all went in the predicted direction. Those who were actively serving in the military would have had lower rates of LCP drug use, as would those who had children, those who were married, those with higher levels of education, and those who worked more hours.

Social Bonds

Indicators of social bonds were included in model 3. Religious participation was the only variable that was significant, for every one unit increase in religious participation there was a 21.1% decrease in LCP drug use, holding constant all other variables in the model (p<.01, IRR = .789).

The next series of models looks at the unique effect of the demographic variables, indicators or turning points, and social bond measures on a sub-sample of the population identified as "persisters." This sub-sample consists of 268 members of the sample who were active AL offenders at wave 2 of the Add Health data and active as AAOs at wave 3 (see Table 27).

Table 30.   *Negative Binomial Regression Models of Persisters on AAO Outcome*

AAO Offending Scale	Model 1			Model 2			Model 3		
	B	(SE)	IRR	B	(SE)	IRR	B	(SE)	IRR
Age	-.080	.057	.923						
Gender	.211	.207	1.23						
Black	.077	.282	1.08						
White	-.008	.256	.992						
Military				-1.76	1.06	.171			
Children				-.175	.248	.839			
Education				.077	.047	1.08			
Hours Worked				-.002	.008	.998			
Married				-.107	.463	.899			
Religious Services							.098	.061	1.10
Economic Instability							.197	.188	1.22
Job Satisfaction							.019	.106	1.01
Parental Attachment							-.137	.085	.871
Property Owned							.241	.217	1.27
Constant							-.665	.417	
*p<.05	Chi – Square = 3.22			Chi – Square = 8.75			Chi – Square = 7.87		
**p<.01	Df = 4			Df = 5			Df = 5		
	Log likelihood = -298.35			Log likelihood = -295.59			Log likelihood = -296.03		
	AIC = 2.27			AIC = 2.25			AIC = 2.26		

The economic instability, parental attachment, and property owned scales were z scored and mean summed.

Demographics

Model 1 included only the demographic variables being controlled for in the analysis. None of the demographic variables were significant in this model. However, it is worth noting that while not significant, some of relationships between the demographic variables and the AAO outcome variables did not go in the predicted directions. Age, as in the majority of the prior analyses presented, went in the expected direction, with an increase in age decreasing the incidence of AAO offending. However, gender (female) was in the opposite direction that was expected. If this variable was significant, females would have had higher rates of AAO offending. While, it is important to note that this finding was not significant, it is still of interest to see that the direction of the finding was not what was expected. Like gender, the race variables also were not in the expected directions, Blacks would have been more likely to commit more AAO offenses, relative to other groups, and whites, as compared to other groups, less likely. As with gender, these variables were not significant, but it is still of interest to see that with persisting offenders, the relationships with the variables changes relative to the (significant) relationships found in analyses containing the full sample.

Turning Points

Indicators of traditional turning points were included into the next model. Of the indicators added, none were significant. While none of the turning point indicators were significant, all went in the predicted direction. Those who were actively serving in the military would have had lower rates of AAO offending, as would those who had children, those who were married, those with higher levels of education, and those who worked more hours.

Social Bonds

None of the indicators of social bond were significant, however, as with the demographic variables discussed above; some of the relationships did not go in the expected directions. Both parental attachment and economic instability went in the expected directions, with stronger parental bonds and increase economic instability positively related to incidence of AAO offending (if significant) . In contrast, job satisfaction, property owned, and religious participation, all went in the opposite direction as expected.

While none of these variables were significant, they did go in the opposite direction as hypothesized, and were not consistent with the results from analyses using the full sample. The next series of models examined the role of demographics, turning points, and social bond in predicting LCP offending for the sub-sample of persisters.

Table 31. *Negative Binomial Regression Models of Persisters on LCP Offending Outcome*

LCP Offenses Scale	Model 1			Model 2			Model 3		
	B	(SE)	IRR	B	(SE)	IRR	B	(SE)	IRR
Age	.012	.033	1.01						
Gender	-.007	.120	.992						
Black	.064	.161	1.07						
White	.036	.146	1.04						
Military				.142	.292	1.15			
Children				-.037	.139	.963			
Education				.002	.029	1.00			
Hours Worked				-.001	.005	.999			
Married				.158	.226	1.17			
Religious Services							.004	.032	1.00
Economic Instability							.021	.091	1.02
Job Satisfaction							-.004	.059	.996
Parental Attachment							-.017	.055	.983
Property Owned							-.034	.095	.966
Constant	-.086	.724		.184	.431		.203	.239	
*p<.05	Chi – Square = 0.31			Chi – Square = 0.83			Chi – Square = 0.99		
**p<.01	Df = 4			Df = 5			Df = 5		
	Log likelihood = -303.66			Log likelihood = -303.40			Log likelihood = -303.64		
	AIC = 2.31			AIC = 2.31			AIC = 2.31		

The economic instability, parental attachment, and property owned scales were z scored and mean summed.

Demographics

Model 1 included only the demographic variables being controlled for in the analysis. None of the demographic variables were significant in this model. However, it is worth noting that while not significant, some of relationships between the demographic variables and the LCP outcome variables did not go in the predicted directions. Age, in contrast to the majority of the prior analyses presented, went in the opposite direction expected, with an increase in age increasing the incidence of LCP offending (if significant). However, gender (female) was in the direction that was expected, with females having lower incidence of LCP offending (if significant). Like age, the race variables also were not in the expected directions, Blacks would have been more likely to commit more LCP offenses, relative to other groups, and whites, as compared to other groups, more likely. As with age, these variables were not significant, but it is still of interest to see that with persisting offenders, the relationships with the variables changes relative to the (significant) relationships found in analyses containing the full sample.

Turning Points

Indicators of traditional turning points were included into the next model. Of the indicators added, none were significant. While none of the turning point indicators were significant, there were some relationships that did not go in the expected direction. Those who were actively serving in the military would have had higher rates of LCP offending, as would those who were married, if significant. The remaining variables, children, education, and hours worked, all went in the expected direction.

Social Bonds

Indicators of social bonds were included in model 3. As with the first 2 models none of the indicators of social bonds were significant. Despite the lack of significance, the direction of the relationship still provides an indication of the possible relationships that exist between these variables and LCP offenses. All of the variables except religious participation were in the predicted direction, having more property owned, stronger bonds with parents, greater levels of religious participation and job satisfaction all would have reduced LCP offenses, if significant. The economic stability variable (reverse scored) was also in the predicted direction, with those having higher levels of instability having greater levels of LCP offenses (if significant). Religious participation went in the opposite direction as expected, with religious participation going in a positive direction. The next series of models examined the role of demographic factors, turning points, and social bonds in predicting AAO drug use for persisters (see Table 29).

Table 32. *Negative Binomial Regression Models of Late Bloomers on AAO Drug Use Outcome*

AAO Drug Use Scale	Model 1			Model 2			Model 3		
	B	(SE)	IRR	B	(SE)	IRR	B	(SE)	IRR
Age	.008	.024	1.01						
Gender	-.029	.086	.971						
Black	-.069	.117	.934						
White	.086	.103	1.09						
Military				-.111	.233	.895			
Children				-.057	.099	.944			
Education				.016	.020	1.02			
Hours Worked				.001	.003	1.01			
Married				.133	.165	1.14			
Religious Services							.001	.023	1.01
Economic Instability							.037	.064	1.04
Job Satisfaction							-.019	.042	.981
Parental Attachment							-.009	.040	.990
Property Owned							.073	.068	1.07
Constant	.696	.517		.673	.305		.959	.168	
*p<.05	Chi – Square = 3.09			Chi – Square = 1.72			Chi – Square = 1.60		
**p<.01	Df = 4			Df = 5			Df = 5		
	Log likelihood = -405.50			Log likelihood = -406.19			Log likelihood = -406.24		
	AIC = 3.06			AIC = 3.07			AIC = 3.07		

The economic instability, parental attachment, and property owned scales were z scored and mean summed.

Poisson regression models were used because of the over dispersion in AAO drug use outcome variable (Long & Freese, 2006; StataCorp, 2006). Three separate models were completed. Model one included demographic variables, age, gender, and two dummy variables capturing the unique effect of race. Model 2 looked at the effects of turning points on crime. Model 3 examined social bonds.

Demographics

Model 1 included only the demographic variables being controlled for in the analysis. None of the demographic variables were significant in this model. However, it is worth noting that while not significant, the relationships between the demographic variables and the AAO drug use outcome were in the expected directions. Age had a negative relationship, suggesting that older offenders would offend less (if significant). Gender was also negative, suggesting females would have lower incidences of AAO drug use. Blacks, as compared to other groups, would have had lower rate of AAO offending. In contrast, whites, compared to other groups, would have had a higher incident rate of AAO drug use.

Turning Points

Indicators of traditional turning points were included into the next model. Of the indicators added, none were significant. While none of the turning point indicators were significant, all went in the predicted direction. Those who were actively serving in the military would have had lower rates of AAO drug use, as would those who had children, those who were married, those with higher levels of education, and those who worked more hours.

Social Bonds

Indicators of social bonds were included in model 3. As with the first 2 models none of the indicators of social bonds were significant. Despite the lack of significance, the direction of the relationship still provides an indication of the possible relationships that exist between these variables and AAO drug use. All of the variables except religious participation were in the predicted direction, having more property owned, stronger bonds with parents, greater levels of religious participation and job satisfaction all would have reduced AAO drugs used, if significant. The economic stability variable (reverse scored) was also in the predicted direction, with those having higher levels of instability having greater levels of AAO drugs used (if significant). Religious participation went in the opposite direction as expected, with religious participation going in a positive direction. The final series of models examined the influence of demographic characteristics, turning points, and social bonds in predicting LCP drug use for persisters (see Table 30).

Table 33. *Negative Binomial Regression Models of Persisters on LCP Drug Use Outcome*

LCP Drug Used Scale	Model 1			Model 2			Model 3		
	B	(SE)	IRR	B	(SE)	IRR	B	(SE)	IRR
Age	.004	.066	1.00						
Gender	-.042	.232	.959						
Black	-.646	.362	.524						
White	.402	.276	1.49						
Military				-.145	1.06	.235			
Children				-.535	.308	.586			
Education				.078	.054	1.08			
Hours Worked				.003	.009	1.00			
Married				.075	.549	1.08			
Religious Services							-.091	.067	.912
Economic Instability							.038	.180	1.04
Job Satisfaction							-.104	.115	.901
Parental Attachment							-.146	.111	.863
Property Owned							.391	.197*	1.48
Constant	-.994	1.45	-1.79	.816			-.243	.449	

*p<.05	Chi – Square = 13.71	Chi – Square = 9.68	Chi – Square = 8.94
**p<.01	Df = 4	Df = 5	Df = 5
	Log likelihood = -233.11	Log likelihood = -235.15	Log likelihood = -235.51
	AIC = 1.78	AIC = 1.80	AIC = 1.8

The economic instability, parental attachment, and property owned scales were z scored and mean summed.

Demographics

Model 1 included only the demographic variables being controlled for in the analysis. None of the demographic variables were significant in this model. However, it is worth noting that while not significant, the relationships between the demographic variables and the LCP drug use outcome were in the expected directions. Age had a negative relationship, suggesting that older offenders would offend less (if significant). Gender was also negative, suggesting females would have lower incidences of LCP drug use. Blacks, as compared to other groups, would have had lower rate of LCP drug use. In contrast, whites, compared to other groups, would have had a higher incident rate of LCP drug use.

Turning Points

Indicators of traditional turning points were included into the next model. Of the indicators added, none were significant. While none of the turning point indicators were significant, there were some relationships that did not go in the expected direction. Those who were married would have had higher rates of LCP drug use, as would those with more education, if significant. The remaining variables, children, military service, and hours worked, all went in the expected direction.

Social Bonds

Indicators of social bonds were included in model 3. Property owned was the only variable that was significant, for every one unit increase in property owned there was a 47% increase in LCP drug use , holding constant all other variables in the model (p<.05, IRR = .863).

References

Aliosi, M. F. (2000). Emerging trends and issues in juvenile justice. In Hancock, B. W., & Sharp, P. M. (Eds.) *Public policy, crime, and criminal justice* (pp. 365-380). Upper Saddle River: Prentice Hall.

Allison, P. A. (2001). *Missing data.* Thousand Oaks, CA: Sage Publications.

Amoatend, A. Y., & Bahr, S. J. (1986). Religion, family, and adolescent drug use. *Sociological Perspectives, 29,* 53-76.

Armour, S., & Haynie, D. L (2007). Sexual Debut and Delinquency. *Journal of Youth and Adolescence, 36,* 141-152.

Arnett, J. J. (1994). Are college students adults? Their conceptions of the transition to adulthood. *Journal of Adult Development, 1,* 154-168.

Arnett, J.J. (1998). Risk behavior and family role transitions during the twenties. *Journal of Youth and Adolescence, 27,* 301-319.

Arnett, J.J. (2000). Emerging adulthood: A theory of development from the late teens through the twenties. *American Psychologist, 55,* 469-480.

Arnett, J. J. (2001). Conceptions of the transition to adulthood: Perspectives from adolescence to middle age. *Journal of Adult Development, 8,* 133-143.

Arnett, J.J. (2005). The developmental context of substance use in emerging adulthood. *The Journal of Drug Issues, 22,* 235-254.

Arnett, J. J. (2006). *Emerging adulthood: The winding road from the late teens through the twenties.* New York: Oxford University Press.

Arnett, J. J., & Tanner, J. L. (2006). (Eds.) *Emergent adults in America.* Washington, D.C.: American Psychological Association.

Bachman, R., & Schutt, R. K. (2007). *The practice of research in criminology and criminal justice* (3rd ed.). Los Angeles, California: Sage Publications.

Baldwin, W. H., & Nord, C. (1984) Delayed child-bearing in the United States: Facts and fictions. *Population Bulletin, 39,* 1-42.

Baltes, P. B. (1968). Longitudinal and cross-sectional sequences in the study of age and generation effects. *Human Development, 11,* 145-171.

Barnes, J.C., & Beaver, K. M. (2010). An empirical examination of adolescent limited offending: A direct test of Moffitt's maturity gap thesis. *Journal of Criminal Justice, 38,* 1176-1185

Baydar, N., & Brooks-Gunn, J. (1998). Profiles of grandmothers who help care for their grandchildren in the United States. *Family Relations, 47,* 385-393.

Beaver, K. M. (2008). Nonshared environmental influences on adolescent delinquent involvement and adult criminal behavior. *Criminology, 46,* 341-370.

Belknap, J. (2007). *The invisible women: Gender, crime and justice* (3rd edition). Belmont, CA: Thomason & Wadsworth Publishers.

Bell, R. Q. (1953). Convergence: An accelerated longitudinal approach. *Child Development, 24,* 145-152.

Bell, N.J.,& Bell, R.W. (1993). *Adolescent risk taking.* Newbury Park, CA: Sage Publications.

Benson, M. L. (2002). *Crime and the life course an introduction.* Los Angeles: Roxbury Publishing.

Berg, I. (1970). *Education and jobs: The great training robbery.* New York: Praeger Publishers.

Beaver, K.M, DeLisi, M., Vaughn, M.G., & Wright, J.P. (2010). The intersection of genes and neuropsychological deficits in the prediction of adolescent delinquency and low self-control. *International Journal of Offender Therapy and Comparative Criminology, 54,* 22-42.

Blalock, H. M. (1966). The identification problem and theory building: The case of status inconsistency. *American Sociological Review, 31,* 52-61.

Blumstein, A. (1995). Youth violence, guns, and the illicit drug industry. *The Journal of Criminal Law and Criminology, 86,* 10-36.

Borsari, B., & Carey, K.B. (2001). Peer influences on college drinking: A review of the research. *Journal of Substance Abuse, 13,* 391-421.

Borsari, B., & Carey, K. B. (2003). Descriptive and injunctive norms in college drinking: A meta- analytic integration. *Journal of Studies on Alcohol, 64,* 331-341.

Boutwell. B.B.. & Beaver. K. M. (2008). A biosocial explanation of delinquency abstention. *Criminal Behavior and Mental Health, 18,* 59-74.

Burtless. G. (1990). In Burtless. G. (Ed.). *A future of lousy jobs? The changing structure of U.S. wages.* Washington DC: The Brookings Institution.

Bryk. A.. & Raudenbush. S.W. (1987). Application of hierarchical models to assessing change. *Psychological Bulletin, 1,* 147-158.

Carey. K. B.. Carey. M. P.. Maisto. S. A.. & J.M. Henson. (2006). Brief motivational interventions for heavy college drinkers: A randomized control trial. *Journal of Consulting and Clinical Psychology, 74,* 943-954.

Chantala. K.. Kalsbeek. W.. & Andraca. E. (2004). Non-response in Wave III of the Add Health study. Retrieved July 23. 2009. from http://www.cpc.unc.edu/projects/addhealth/files/W3nonres.pdf.

Chantala. K . & Tabor. J. (1999). Strategies to perform a design based analysis using the Add Health Data. Retrieved July 23. 2009. from http://www.cpc.unc.edu/projects/addhealth/files/weight1.pdf.

Champion. D. J.. Hartley. R. D.. & Rabe. G.A. (2008). *Criminal courts structure, process, and issues* (2nd ed.). Upper Saddle River. NJ: Prentice Hall Publishers.

Chassin. L.. Pitts. S. C.. & Prost. J. (2002). Binge drinking trajectories from adolescence to emerging adulthood in a high risk sample: Predictors and substance abuse outcomes. *Journal of Consulting and Clinical Psychology, 70,* 68-78.

Chen. K. & Kandel. D. B. (1995). The natural history of drug use from adolescence to the mid-thirties in a general population sample. *American Journal of Public Health, 85,* 41-47. Cote. J. (2000). *Arrested adulthood: The changing nature of maturity and identity.* New York: New York University Press.

Cote. J. E.. & Allhar. A. (1995). *Generation on hold: Coming of age in the late twentieth century.* New York: New York University Press.

Cronbach. L. J. (1951). Coefficient alpha and the internal structure of tests. *Psychometrika, 16,* 297-334.

Cronbach. L. J. (1970). *Essentials of psychological testing* (3rd edition). New York: Harper & Row Publishers.

Darlington. R. B. (1990). *Regression and linear models.* Columbus. OH: McGraw Hill Publications.

Dempster, A. P., Rubin, D.b., & Tsutakawa, R. K. (1981). Estimation in covariance components models. *Journal of the American Statistical Association, 76,* 341-353.

Elder, G. H. (1985). Perspectives on the life course. In Elder, G.H. *Life course dynamics: Trajectories and transitions, 1968-1980,* 23-49. Ithaca, NY: Cornell University Press.

Elder, G. H. (1998). The life course and developmental theory. *Child development, 69,* 1-12.

Ellickson, P.L., Collins, R. L., & Bell, R.M. (1999). Adolescent use of illicit drugs other than marijuana: How important is social bonding and for which ethnic group? *Substance use and misuse, 34,* 317-346.

Elliott, D. D. (1994). Serious violent offenders: Onset, developmental course, and termination the American society of criminology 1993 presidential address. *Criminology, 32,* 1-21.

Elliott, D. S., Huizinga, D., & Ageton, S. S. (1985). *Explaining delinquency and drug use.* Beverly Hills, CA: Sage Publications.

Elliott, D. S., Huizinga, D., & Menard, S. (1989). *Multiple problem youth: Delinquency, drugs and mental health problems.* New York: Springer Publications.

Elliot, D. S., & Voss, H. L. (1974). *Delinquency and Dropout.* Lexington, MA: D.C. Heath Publications.

Espenshade, T. J. (1985). Marriage trends in America: Estimates, implications, and underlying causes. *Population and Development Review, 11,* 193-245.

Fabio, A., Loeber, R., Balasubramani, G.K., Roth, J., Fu, W., & Farrington, D. (2006). Why some generations are more violent than others: Assessment of age, period, and cohort effects. *American Journal of Epidemiology, 164,* 151-160.

Fagin, J. A. (2007). *Criminal justice 2ⁿᵈ edition.* Upper Saddle River, NJ: Prentice Hall Publishers.

Farrington, D. (1986). Age and crime. In Tonry, M. & Morris, N. (Eds). *Crime and justice: An annual review of research.* Volume 7, 189-250, Chicago: University of Chicago Press.

Farrington, D. P., Ohlin, L.E., & Wilson, J. Q. (1986). *Understanding and controlling crime: Toward a new research strategy.* New York: Springer Publications.

Felson, R. B., & Haynie, D. L. (2002). Pubertal development, social factors, and delinquency amount adolescent boys. *Criminology, 40,* 967-988.

Fletcher, J., & Wolfe, B. (2008). Child mental health and human capital accumulation: The case of ADHD revisited. *Journal of Health Economics, 27,* 794-800.

Gills, A. M., & Michaels, R. (1992). Does drug use lower wages? *Industrial and Labor Relations Review, 45,* 419-434.

Goldscheider, F., & Goldscheider, C. (1994). Leaving and returning home in twentieth century America. *Population Reference Bulletin, 48,* 1-35.

Gottfredson, M. R., & Hirschi, T. (1990). *A general theory of crime.* Stanford, CA: Stanford University Press.

Gutmann, M. P., Pullum-Pinon, S. M., & Pullum, T. W. (2002). Three eras of young adults home leaving in twentieth century America. *Journal of Social History, 35,* 533-576.

Guo, G., Roettger, M.E., & Cai, T. (2008). The integration of genetic propensities into social control models of delinquency and violence among males. *American Sociological Review, 72,* 543-568.

Harris, K. M., Francesca F., Tabor, J., Bearman, P.S., Jones, J, & Udry, J. R. (2003). The National Longitudinal Study of Adolescent Health: Research Design [WWW document]. URL: http://www.cpc.unc.edu/projects/addhealth/design.

Haynie, D. L. (2003). Contexts of risk? Explaining the link between girls pubertal development and their delinquency involvement. *Social Forces, 82,* 355-397.

Haynie, D. L., Giordano, P., Manning, W., & Longmore, M. (2005). Gender, romance, and delinquency involvement. *Criminology, 43,* 177-210.

Haynie, D. L., & McHugh, S. (2003). Sibling Delinquency: In the shadows of mutual and unique friendship effects? *Criminology, 41,* 355-392.

Haynie, D. L., South, S. J. & Bose, S. (2006a). Residential mobility and attempted suicide among adolescents: An individual-level Analysis. *Sociological Quarterly, 47,* 693-721.

Haynie, D. L., South, S. J, & Bose, S. (2006b). The company you keep: Adolescent mobility and peer behavior. *Sociological Inquiry, 76,* 397-426.

Haynie, D. L., & Osgood, W. L. (2005). Reconsidering peers and delinquency: How do peers matter? *Social Forces, 84,* 1109-1130.

Haynie, D. L., & Payne, D. (2006). Race, friendship networks, and violent delinquency. *Criminology, 4*, 775-806.

Haynie, D. L., & Piquero, A. (2006). Pubertal development and victimization risk: Differences across gender. *Journal of Research in Crime and Delinquency, 43*, 3-35.

Haynie, D. L., Silver, E., & Teasdale. B.(2006). Neighborhood characteristics, peer influence, and adolescent violence. *Journal of Quantitative Criminology, 22*, 147-169.

Haynie, D., Weiss, H., & Piquero, A. (2008). Race, the economic maturity gap, and criminal offending in young adulthood. *Justice Quarterly, 25*, 595-622.

Hilbe, J. M. (2008). *Negative binomial regression*. New York: Cambridge University Press.

Hirschi, T. (1969). *Causes of delinquency*. Berkley, CA: University of California Press.

Hirschi, T., & Gottfredson, M. (1983). Age and the explanation of crime. *American Journal of Sociology, 89*, 552-582.

Huizinga, D., Menard, S., & Elliott, D. S. (1989). Delinquency and drug use: Temporal and developmental patterns. *Justice Quarterly, 6*, 419-455.

Jennings, W. G., Maldonado-Molina, M. M., Piquero, A. R., Odgers, C.L., Bird, H., & Caninio, G. (2010). Sex differences in trajectories of offending among Puerto Rican youth. *Crime & Delinquency, 56*, 327-357.

Laird, N.M., & Ware, J. H. (1982). Random-effects models for longitudinal data. *Biometrics, 38*, 963- 974.

Jackson, K.M., Sher, K. J., & Park, A. Drinking among college students: Consumption and consequences. In Galanter, M. (Ed). *Recent developments in alcoholism: Alcohol problems in adolescents and young adults*, 85-117. New York: Springer Publications.

Jensen, L. A., Arnett, J. J., Feldman, S. S., & Cauffmann, E. (2004). The right to do wrong: Lying to parents among adolescents and emerging adults. *Journal of Youth and Adolescence, 33*, 101-112.

Jessor, R., Donovan, J.E., & Costa, F.M. (1991). *Beyond adolescence: Problem behavior and young adult development*. New York: Cambridge University Press.

Katz, L. F. (1994). Active labor market policies to expand employment and opportunity. *Proceedings, Jan*, 239-322.

Kypri, K., McCarthy, D., Coe, M., & Brown, S. (2004). Transition to independent living and substance involvement. *Journal of Child & Adolescent Substance Abuse, 13*, 85-100.

Kohlberg, L. (1981). *The psychology of moral development: The nature and validity of moral stages.* New York: Harper & Row Publishers.

Laub, J. H., & Sampson, R. J. (1993). Turning points in the life course: Why change matters in the study of crime. *Criminology, 31*, 301-325.

Laub, J. H., & Samson, R. J. (2001).Understanding desistance from crime. *Crime and Justice, 28*, 1-69.

Laub, J. H., & Sampson, R. J. (2003). *Shared beginnings, divergent lives: Delinquent boys to age 70.* Cambridge, MA: Harvard University Press.

Lochner, L., & Moretti, E. (2001). *The effect of education on crime: Evidence from prison inmates, arrests, and self-reports. JCPR Working Paper #287.* Chicago: Joint Center for Poverty Research, Northwestern University/University of Chicago.

Lochner, L.. & Moretti, E. (2004). The effect of education on crime: Evidence from prison inmates, arrestees, and self reports. *The American Economic Review, 94*, 155 – 189.

Long, J. S., & Freese, J. (2006). *Regression models for categorical dependent variables using STATA (2nd edition).* College, Station, Texas: Stata Press.

Maldonado-Molina, M.M., Piquero, A. R., Jennings, W.G., Bird, H., & Canino, G. (2009). Trajectories of delinquency among Puerto Rican children and adolescents and Two Sites. *Journal of Research in Crime and Delinquency, 46*, 144-181.

Marion, N. E., & Oliver, W. M. (2006). *The public policy of crime and criminal justice.* Upper Saddle River, NJ: Prentice Hall Publishers.

Mason, K.O., Mason, W.M., Winsborough, H. H., & Poole, W. K. (1973). Some methodological issues in cohort analysis of archival data. *American Sociological Review, 38*, 242-258.

Menard, S. (1992). Demographic and theoretical variables in the age-period-cohort analysis of illegal behavior. *Journal of Research in Crime and Delinquency, 29*, 178-199.

Merton, R. K. (1938). Social structure and anomie. *American Sociological Review, 3*, 672 – 682.

Mirel, J. E. (1991). Adolescence in Twentieth-century America. In Learner, R. M., Peterson, A. C., & Brooks-Gunn J. *Encyclopedia of Adolescence*. New York: Garland Press.

Mroczek, D. K., & Spirio, A. (2005). Changes in life satisfaction during adulthood: Findings from the veterans affairs normative aging study. *Journal of Personality and Social Psychology, 88*, 189-202.

Moffitt, T. E. (1993). Adolescence limited and life course persistent antisocial behavior: A developmental taxonomy. *Psychological Review, 100*, 674-701.

Moffitt, T.E. (2006). A review of research on taxonomy of life course persistent versus adolescent limited antisocial behavior in Cullen, F.T., Wright, J.P, & Blevins, K.R. (pp.277-311). *Taking stock: the status of criminological theory.* New Brunswick, NJ: Transaction Publishers.

Moffitt, T. E., Caspi, A., Rutter, M., & Silva, P.A. (2001). *Sex differences in antisocial behavior: Conduct disorder, delinquency, and violence in the Dunedin longitudinal study.* New York: Cambridge University Press.

Moffitt, T. E., Caspi, A., Harrington, H., & Milne, B.J. (2002). Males on the life-course persistent and adolescent-limited anti-social pathways: Follow up at age 26 years. *Development and Psychopathology, 14*, 179-207.

Moran, M. D. (2003). Arguments for rejecting the sequential Bonferroni in ecological studies. *Oikas, 100*, 403-405.

Mumola, C. J., & Karberg, J. C. (2006, October [revised January 19, 2007]). *Drug use and dependence, State and federal prisoners, 2004* (NCJ 213530, BJS Special Report). Washington,DC: U.S. Department of Justice, Office of Justice Programs, Bureau of Justice Statistics.National Center for Education Statistics. Http://nces.ed.gov/programs/digest/d05/tables/dt05_181.asp. Accessed December 01, 2007.

National Household Survey on Drug Use and Health, 2005. (2007). *Results from the 2005 national survey on drug use and health: National findings.* Deparament of Health and Human Surveys Substance Abuse and Mental Health Services Administration (SAMSA). Washington DC.

Normand, J., Lempert, R., O., & O'Brien, C. P. (Eds.). (1994). *Under the influence? Drugs and the American work force.* Washington, DC: National Academy.

Norusis, M.J. (2002). *SPSS 11.0 Guide to data analysis.* Upper Saddle River, NJ: Prentice Hall Publishers.

Nunnally, J.C. (1978). *Psychometric theory (2nd edition)*. New York: McGraw Hill Publishers.

O'Brien, R. M. (2000). Age period cohort characteristics models. *Social Science Research, 29*, 123-139.

Okimoto, J. D., & Stegall, P. J. (1987). *Boomerang kids*. New York, New York: Simon & Schuster Publishers.

O'Malley, P. M., Bachman, J. G., & Johnston, L. D. (1984). Period, age, and cohort effects on substance use among American youth, 1976-1982. *American Journal of Public Health, 74*, 682-688.

Pallant, J. (2007). *SPSS survival manual (3rd edition)*. New York: McGraw Hill Publications.

Palmore, E. (1978). When can age, period and cohort be separated? *Social Forces, 57*, 282-295.

Pearce, L. D., & Haynie, D. L.(2004). Intergenerational religious dynamics and adolescent delinquency. *Social Forces, 82*, 1553-1572.

Pebley, A.R., & Rudkin, L.L. (1999). Grandparents caring for grandchildren: What do we know? *Journal of Family Issues, 20*, 218-242.

Perneger, T.V. (1998). What's wrong with Bonferroni adjustments. *British Medical Journal, 316*, 1236-1238.

Peters, K. (2007). Protecting the millennial college student. *Southern California Review of Law and Social Justice*, Spring, 431- 468.

Piquero, A. R., Brame, R., Mazerolle, P. & Haapanen, R. (2002). Crime in emerging adulthood. *Criminology, 40*, 137-169.

Piquero, A. R., Farrington, D., & Blumstein, A. (2007). *Key Issues in Criminal Career Research: New Analyses from the Cambridge Study in Delinquent Development*. New York: Cambridge University Press.

Pratt, T.C., & Cullen, F.T. (2000). The empirical status of Gottfredson and Hirschi's general theory of crime: A meta-analysis. *Criminology, 35*, 157-174.

Puzzanchera, C. (2009). Juvenile Arrests 2007. *Juvenile Justice Bulletin*. Washington, DC. Office of Juvenile Justice and Delinquency Prevention.

Quattrocchi, M.M., & Golden, C.J. (1983). Peabody picture vocabulary test-revised and Luria-Nebraska neuropsychological battery for children: Intercorrelations for normal youngsters. *Perceptual and Motor Skills, 56*, 632-634.

Richard, A.J., Bell, D.C., & Carlson, J.W. (2000). Individual religiosity, moral community, and drug treatment. *Journal for the Scientific Study or Religion, 39*, 240-246.

Rohrbach, L. A., Sussman, S. Dent, C.W., & Sun, P. (2005). Tobacco, alcohol, and other drug use among high risk young people: A five year longitudinal study from adolescence to emerging adulthood. *The Journal of Drug Issues, 22*, 333-356.

Ryder, N. B. (1965). The cohort as a concept in the study of change. *American Sociological Review, 30*, 843-861.

Salvatore, C., & Welsh, W. (2008). *The emergence of the arrested adolescent.* Paper presentation at the American Society of Criminology Conference, St. Louis, Missouri 2008.

Salvatore, C., & Welsh, W. (2009). *The emergence of the arrested adolescent offender.* Unpublished manuscript.

Sampson, R. J., & Laub, J. H. (2005). *Crime in the making: Pathways and turning points through life.* Harvard University Press.

Sampson, R.J., Laub, J.H., & Wimer, C. (2006). Does marriage reduce crime? A counterfactual approach to within – individual causal effects. *Criminology, 44*, 465 – 507.

Sargent, J. (1986). An improving job market for college graduates: The 1986 update of projections to 1995 *Occupational Outlook Quarterly, 30*, 3-7.

Schafer, J.L. (1997). *Imputation of missing covariates under a general linear mixed model.* Technical report, Department of Statistics, Pennsylvania State University.

Shifren, K., Furnham, A., & Bauserman, R. L. (2003). Emerging adulthood in American and British samples: Individuals' personality and health risk behaviors. *Journal of Adult Development, 10*, 75-87.

Singer, J.D., & Willett, J. B. (2003). *Applied longitudinal data analysis: Modeling change and event occurrence.* New York: Oxford University Press.

Soothill, K., Francis, B., Ackerley, E., & Humphreys, L. (2007). *British Journal of Criminology,* Ahead of Print.

StataCorp. (2006). *Stata statistical software: Release 9.* College Station, TX: StataCorp.

Steffensmeier, D., Streifel, C., Harer, M. D. (1987). Relative cohort size and youth crime in the United States, 1953-1984. *American Sociological Review, 52*, 702-710.

Steinberg, L. (2005). Cognitive and affective development in adolescence. *Trends in Cognitive Sciences, 9*, 69-75.

Sternio, J. L. F. Weisburg, H. I., & Bryk, A.S. (1983). Empirical Bayes estimation of individual growth curve parameters and their relationships to covariates. *Biometrics, 39*, 71-86.

Stevens, J. (1996). *Applied multivariate statistics for the social sciences* (3rd Ed). Mahway, NJ: Lawrence Erlbaum Publishers.

South, S.J., & Haynie, D. L. (2004). Friendship networks of mobile adolescents. *Social Forces, 83*, 315-350.

SPSS Missing Value Analysis 16.0. (2007). SPSS Inc. Chicago, Il.

Taylor, R. B (1994). *Research methods in criminal justice.* Columbus, OH: McGraw Hill.

Thornberry, T. P. (Ed.) (1997). *Developmental theories of crime and delinquency.* New Brunswick, NJ: Transaction Publishers.

Thorndike, R. L. (Ed). (1971). *Educational measurement* (2nd ed.). Washington D.C., American Council on Education.

Tonry, M. Ohlin, L.E., & Farrington, D. P. (1991). *Human development and criminal behavior: New ways of advancing knowledge.* New York: Springer Verlag Publishers.

Tucker, J. S., Ellickson, P. L., Orlando, M., Martino, S. C., & Klein, D. J. (2005). Substance use trajectories from early adolescence to emerging adulthood: A comparison of smoking, binge drinking, and marijuana use. *Journal of Drug Issues, 22*, 307-332.

Udry, J. R. (1998). The National Longitudinal Study of Adolescent Health (Add Health), Waves I & II, 1994–1996 [machine-readable data file and documentation]. Chapel Hill, NC: Carolina Population Center, University of North Carolina at Chapel Hill.

Udry, J. R. (2003). The National Longitudinal Study of Adolescent Health (Add Health), Wave III, 2001–2002 [machine-readable data file and documentation]. Chapel Hill, NC: Carolina Population Center, University of North Carolina at Chapel Hill.

U.S. Bureau of Census. (1972). *Marital status and living arrangements: March 1972.* Current Population reports, Series P-20, 242. Washington, DC: U.S. Government Printing Office.

U.S. Bureau of Census. (1988). *Marital status and living arrangements: March 1987.* Current Population reports, Series P-20, 423. Washington, DC: U.S. Government Printing Office.

Ware, J. H. (1985). Linear models for the analysis of longitudinal studies. *Journal of the American Statistical Association, 80,* 95-101.

Welsh, W. (2001). Effects of student and school factors on five measures of school disorder. *Justice Quarterly, 18,* 911-947.

White, H. R. & Jackson, K. (2004). Social and psychological influences on emerging adult drinking behavior. *Alcohol Research & Health, 28,* 182-190.

White, H. R., Labouvie, E. W., & Papadaratasakis, V. (2005). Changes in substance use during the transition to adulthood: A comparison of college students and their non-college age peers. *Journal of Drug Issues, 22,* 281-306.

White, H.R., McMorris, B.J., Catalano, R.F., Fleming, C.B., Haggerty, & Abbott, R. D. (2006). Increases in alcohol and marijuana use during the transition out of high school into emerging adulthood: The effects of leaving home, going to college, and high school protective factors. *Journal of Studies on Alcohol, 67,* 810-822.

Wilkie, J. R. (1981). The trend toward delayed parenthood. *Journal of Marriage and the Family, 43,* 583-591.

Wilkinson, B. (1951). A statistical consideration in psychology research. *Psychological Bulletin, 48,* 56-158.

William T. Grant Foundation. (1988). *The forgotten half: Non-college youth in America.* Washington, DC: William T. Grant Foundation.

Wilson, W.J. (1987). *The truly disadvantaged: The inner city, the underclass, and public policy.* Chicago: University of Chicago Press.

Wilson, W.J. (1996). *When work disappears: The world of the new urban poor.* New York: Random House Press.

Wright, J.P., Beaver, K. M., DeLisi, M., & Vaughn, M.G. (2008). Evidence of negligible parenting influences on self-control, delinquent peers, and delinquency in a sample of twins. *Justice Quarterly, 25,* 544-569

Wright, J. P., Carter, D. E., & Cullen, F. T. (2005). A life course analysis of military service in Vietnam. *Journal of Research in Crime and Delinquency, 42,* 55-83.

Yang, Y. (2008). Social inequalities in happiness in the United States, 1972 to 2004: An age-period- cohort analysis. *American Sociological Review, 73,* 204-226.

Yang, Y., & Land., K.C. (2007). A mixed models approach to the age-period-cohort analysis of repeated cross-sections surveys, with an applications to data on trends in verbal test scores. *Sociological Methodology, 36,* 75-97.

This research uses data from Add Health, a program project directed by Kathleen Mullan Harris and designed by J. Richard Udry, Peter S. Bearman, and Kathleen Mullan Harris at the University of North Carolina at Chapel Hill, and funded by grant P01-HD31921 from the Eunice Kennedy Shriver National Institute of Child Health and Human Development, with cooperative funding from 23 other federal agencies and foundations. Special acknowledgment is due Ronald R. Rindfuss and Barbara Entwisle for assistance in the original design. Information on how to obtain the Add Health data files is available on the Add Health website (http://www.cpc.unc.edu/addhealth). No direct support was received from grant P01-HD31921 for this analysis.

Index

CPSIA information can be obtained at www.ICGtesting.com
Printed in the USA
BVOW05*1409090215

386493BV00001BA/1/P